One Journey to a Final Destiny

One Journey to a Final Destiny

OUR JOURNEY FROM BEGINNING TO END

MINISTER SARA JUICE & DR. ABRAM JUICE

PRIMIX PUBLISHING
THE WRITE CHOICE

Primix Publishing
East Brunswick Office Evolution
1 Tower Center Boulevard, Ste 1510
East Brunswick, NJ 08816
www.primixpublishing.com
Phone: 1-800-538-5788

Published by Primix Publishing: 04/10/2026

ISBN: 979-8-89194-505-0(sc)
ISBN: 979-8-89194-506-7(e)

Library of Congress Control Number: 2025912012

Contents

Part 1

Part 2

Part 1

One Journey to A Final Destiny

This book is about our life's journey — the path that God has prepared for each of us. Before our lives became intertwined, we each had our own individual lifestyle and walk of faith. It was during that time that the Spirit of the Lord moved upon my husband's heart to write *"Where Do We Go from Here?"*

That question in itself is powerful — one that calls for deep reflection. When you feel you have done everything you can, you begin to ask, *"What's next? Who do I turn to now?"* The answer is **Jesus**. If we start our journey with Christ from the very beginning, those questions would not weigh so heavily on our hearts.

In 2019, we began our journey together and became united in one love. The title of this book, *One Journey to a Final Destiny*, was placed in my heart by God even before our union. It reminds us that we each have a journey to travel in this life. Yet, because God has given us free will, the question remains: **What will be your final destiny?**

Choose obedience and you will eat the good of the land. As it is written in **Isaiah 1:19**, *"If you are willing and obedient, you will eat the good of the land."*

This journey is about the power of choice — choosing **life or death** for your life. It is about surrendering to God's will, joining together as one, and allowing the **Holy Spirit** to lead and guide us under one umbrella of faith, love, and divine purpose.

Dr. Jerome D. Brown and Tonya Brown's Story

The weary hearts and souls of my book *Where Do We Go from Here*, and *I See Restoring Peace from God's Point of View* are based on biblical principles, values, and the Word of God, as a tribute to the courage and character of all crime victims.

My work as an ordained minister of the Gospel of Jesus Christ and a certified Christian counselor reflects my commitment to God's calling. I, **Dr. Jerome D. Brown, D.N.C.**, have been a registered student at **Shalom Bible College & Seminary** since August 28, 2005. I completed my **Bachelor of Divinity degree** in February 2010, graduating with honors (*cum laude*). In June 2011, I completed my **Master's Degree in Theology** with high honors (*magna cum laude*), and in June 2014, I completed the **Doctoral Program in Nouthetic Counseling (Christian Counseling)**.

At present, I am enrolled in the **Ph.D. in Philosophy program** and remain in excellent standing with **Shalom Bible College and Seminary**, a ministry of West Des Moines, Iowa. The institution is accredited by the **American Accrediting Association of Theological Institutions**—a Christian, not secular, accrediting body dedicated to religious education and theological studies.

I am also a member of **Commence Community Church** in West Des Moines, Iowa. The Ph.D. in Philosophy program focuses on the discussion of **Theology vs. Philosophy**, emphasizing **Christian counseling using the Word of God**.

Over the years, I have served in **prison ministry, Kairos, and various churches in Free world**, alongside my late pastor and brother, **Rev. Percy T. Brown Sr.** I have worked in the ministry since the age of twelve, which has helped me develop empathy for offenders, Christians, and others alike.

I do not excuse my own offenses or those of others; however, I now understand many of the influences that have shaped both my behavior and that of others. I have learned to condemn wrongful actions while still recognizing the goodness that exists within the hearts and minds of individuals, including those who are incarcerated.

(See Genesis 24:12–52; Acts 12:5–12; 1 Timothy 2:1–2; Acts 10:1–23; Luke 23:42–43; Habakkuk 3:1–19; 1:1–4; 2 Chronicles 14:11.)

Tonya's Story and Testimony

My name is **Tonya Brown**, and I am a true and faithful believer in **Jesus Christ**. I want to share my life story with you — but first, I must say that **God is my testimony**. Without Him, I wouldn't have a story to tell, and I wouldn't be here today.

God is so good and awesome that I hardly know where to begin. I was raised to know and love our Lord and Savior. At the age of **17**, I made a conscious decision to accept **Jesus Christ** as my Lord and Savior — not because anyone made me, but because I was chosen by His Spirit. I felt I was old enough to make that decision for myself, so I did.

By that time, I had already begun walking in sin and had two children, two years apart. This was only the beginning of my journey — a lot has happened between then and now.

My Journey Through Trials and Healing

2013 – I suffered **five mini-strokes**.

2014 (February 28) – I experienced my **sixth stroke** and a **brain aneurysm**, which caused bleeding from my right eye.

2019 – I **surrendered my whole self to God** and began walking in my deliverance.

2020 – The Spirit taught me to **let go and let God**, walking by faith and not by sight.

2021 – God began teaching me to **walk in the newness and wholeness of the Holy Spirit**.

My Healing Process

God gave me a divine process of healing that took **15 months (1 year and 3 months)** — one day at a time with Jesus:

1. **First 3 months:** Airing out
2. **Second 3 months:** Withdrawal
3. **Third 3 months:** Recovery
4. **Fourth 3 months:** Deliverance
5. **Fifth 3 months:** Overcomer

Through this process, God drew me closer to Him — strengthening me spiritually, mentally, and emotionally.

A Life Restored

By the age of **21**, I had two more children. At **28**, I got married, but on **November 17, 1999**, the state took custody of my children. That loss broke me deeply, and for years I wrestled with pain and confusion.

By the age of **34**, I began to do some serious soul-searching and made a total commitment to walk with God. I wanted to be free from an unequally yoked marriage and be reunited with my children. Between the ages of **34 and 36**, I developed a remarkable and intimate relationship with God.

It was during this season that the Spirit of the Lord inspired me to write **"Sleepless Nights and Awakened Moments."**

Through every trial — from sickness to loss to deliverance — God has been my strength and my healer. My story is a living testimony that **no matter where you are or what you've been through, God can restore, heal, and use your life for His glory.**

Jerome's Testimony

This is my testimony — how I was brought to where I am today and how I became who I am: **Dr. Jerome Diego Brown**. I began preaching at the age of 12 in Fort Worth, Texas. From that early start, I ministered to my peers and other pastors, preaching the gospel. This journey eventually led me to write my book.

My book is about **my life**, what I am called to do with it, and how I can help myself, my community, and others. The subject of my testimony reflects my experiences and the lessons that brought me to ask the question: *"Where Do We Go From Here?"* My life experiences have given me hope, and my desire is now to share that hope with others.

Hope without faith isn't possible. To please God, we must come to Him and believe that He rewards those who seek Him. Some may not have sought Him, but I did, and that pursuit led me to the writing of this book.

One Journey to a Final Destiny is the title of my book. It reflects my sacrifices, struggles, visions, dreams, and insights into the Word of God and prophecy over my life and the lives of others. Through this journey, I realized that **we all have a journey and a destiny**.

As I attended Bible college, I learned to think, pray, and believe that there is a God. I came to know the Savior — **our Lord and Savior, Jesus Christ** — and understood that we must believe, seek Him, and allow Him to guide our lives. It was during this time that God brought my wife into my life. She was also on the verge of writing her book, and together we combined our insights into one shared vision.

One Journey to a Final Destiny tells the story of my life, her life, and the lives of others so that readers can understand that **we all have one journey to a final destiny**. Eternity awaits us, and the choice is ours — heaven or hell. My prayer is that readers will **choose by faith to**

follow Jesus Christ as Lord, so they can truly answer the question: *"Where Do We Go From Here?"*

This book is about the **healing process of a wounded warrior**. It is my hope and prayer that through reading it, others will find direction, encouragement, and the assurance that **their labor is not in vain.**

Tonya's End Sermon: Change / Peeling Back the Layers

Abba, Father, has a way of stripping us down to our **nakedness without touching us**. We may come to Him for physical needs, but when it's all over, He has worked in us and allowed us to understand His Word:

Philippians 4:19 – *"But my God shall supply all your need according to His riches in glory by Christ Jesus."*
God cares about **all our needs**.

Philippians 4:13 – *"I can do all things through Christ who strengthens me."*

These verses remind us that as believers, we can call on the Lord, and He will answer us in **any circumstance or situation in life** — whether in suffering or abundance — with **contentment and peace**.

Change is a necessity in our lives, and it is also a **process to progress**. We must allow the layers of our hearts and lives to be **peeled back and uncovered**, realizing that sin exists — but sin can be forgiven and corrected.

Ask yourself: Are you ready to **clean up what you have messed up?** Give it to God and allow Him to help you **start over again**. Remember, it's about **change and peeling back those layers**.

This short sermon came from a **mess that became a message** and a **test that turned into a testimony.**

One Journey to A Final Destiny

MOPMKIP Outreach Ministries: Ministering in Many Streams

Founder: Dr. Bishop Jerome D. Brown
Co-Founder: Minister Evangelist Tonya Brown

MOPMKIP stands for **Messenger of Peace / Mission Kingdom Inner Peace.**

Our Mission Statement

Our desire is to meet people right where they are — to teach them to reach one, and to teach one how to become a unity of one, all in the mighty name of **Jesus Christ**.

Our goal is to feed people both **physically and spiritually** — to provide natural food for the body and the Word of God for the soul, so that each person may grow from the inside out.

We envision an **Outreach Community Center** that provides:

- **Clothing and Food** for those in need
- **Bible Classes** that teach the Word of God and how to apply it in daily living
- **Arts and Crafts Programs**
- **Cooking and Meal Preparation Classes**

As part of this ministry, we serve the hungry, counsel the broken, and uplift those who seek hope. We also host a fellowship program called **"Men and Women of Wisdom: Walking in Purpose,"** a roundtable ministry that encourages open conversation, spiritual growth, and mutual support.

The Journey of Ministering

Dr. Bishop Jerome D. Brown began his walk with God at the age of 13. In 2012, he fully answered his calling to the **Gospel of Peace**. He pursued his studies at **Shalom Bible College and Seminary**, where he earned his **Doctorate in Ministry**.

Minister Evangelist Tonya Brown began her walk with God at the age of 15. On **March 22, 2019**, she surrendered her all to God and answered her divine calling. On **May 12, 2019**, she was ordained by her husband, **Dr. Bishop Jerome D. Brown**.

Together, they have two living daughters, three grandchildren, and are expecting their first set of twins together. They also lovingly remember their two sons who passed away, one year apart. The Browns have been married for **six years**, during which they also **united their ministries into one — MOPMKIP Outreach Ministries**.

The Meaning Behind the Names

Messenger of Peace — founded by **Dr. Bishop Jerome D. Brown** — draws its inspiration from **Esther 9:29–32**, where Queen Esther and Mordecai sent letters of peace and confirmation throughout the kingdom. This name symbolizes the divine calling to bring peace, restoration, and unity to God's people.

Mission Kingdom Inner Peace — founded by **Minister Evangelist Tonya Brown** — was birthed from her experience as both an **entrepreneur** and an **ambassador for Christ**, representing inner peace through faith and purpose.

When these two ministries united, they became **MOPMKIP Outreach Ministries — Ministering in Many Streams**, a divine partnership dedicated to serving, healing, teaching, and leading others to Christ.

Chapter 1

SLEEPLESS NIGHTS AND AWAKENED MOMENTS

There are times in our lives when we experience sleepless nights — when we toss and turn, unable to rest, with thoughts constantly running through our minds.

Sleepless nights often come when we are reflecting and wondering: *If I had tried it this way or that way... if I had said it differently... would it have made a difference?*

We are **spirit, body, and soul**. God first created us with a spirit, then formed a body over that spirit, and finally gave us a soul to unite them both. Each part — spirit, body, and soul — works together in harmony, according to God's divine design.

The book of **Genesis** speaks of the beginning of God's creation. The Spirit of God existed then, exists now, and will always exist — even within us. God's plan was to place flesh upon the spirit, that we might have physical form — to be seen, to be heard, and to carry out His will and purpose here on earth.

Giving Honor to God

First, giving all honor to our **Heavenly Father**, to **Jesus Christ His Son**, and to the **Holy Spirit**, we are reminded of **1 Corinthians 13:11–12 (KJV):**

> *"When I was a child, I spake as a child, I understood as a child, I thought as a child: but when I became a man, I put away childish things.*
>
> *For now we see through a glass, darkly; but then face to face: now I know in part; but then shall I know even as also I am known."*

This scripture reminds us that as we grow spiritually, we begin to see more clearly the truth of who we are in Christ — no longer in confusion, but in revelation.

Awakened Moments

This is the **awakening of the spirit being** within you. Prepare your heart for what you are about to receive. You are being awakened to the **Light of the World**, which is the true **Word of God** — spiritual nourishment and food for thought during your time of meditation.

Matthew 6:33 (KJV):

> *"But seek ye first the kingdom of God, and his righteousness; and all these things shall be added unto you."*

We must meditate on His Word daily to keep our pathways straight and our minds focused on His truth.

God has placed a **new dominion and authority** over our lives. Challenges may come, but each challenge will bring forth change — in **Jesus' name!**

The Meaning of Awakening

Noun: an act or moment of becoming suddenly aware of something.

Adjective: coming into existence or awareness.

A Call to Reflection

We have been chosen by God. This is the anointed and appointed time. Ask yourself these questions:

1. Are you connected with God?
2. Do you have a relationship with Him?
3. Do you spend quality time with God?
4. Are you abiding in His Word?
5. Do you place limitations on God?
6. Do you meditate on His Word day and night?

Reflect deeply on each of these questions, and make a decision to draw nearer to Him. The Word tells us, *"My people are destroyed for lack of knowledge"* (**Hosea 4:6**). Therefore, keep the statutes of God, and obey all His commandments.

Meditate and Prosper

Joshua 1:8 (KJV):

> *"This book of the law shall not depart out of thy mouth;*
> *but thou shalt meditate therein day and night,*
> *that thou mayest observe to do according to all that is*
> *written therein:*
> *for then thou shalt make thy way prosperous, and then*
> *thou shalt have good success."*

Let your sleepless nights become **awakened moments** — times of divine reflection, spiritual growth, and renewed faith in God's promises.

Chapter 2

THERE IS A SPIRITUAL WAR GOING ON!

God has given us a position on the battlefront!
Men and women everywhere face challenges that threaten to overwhelm them and their loved ones.

A child's destructive behavior and poor choices.
Broken marriages.
Bad medical reports.
Depression, fear, anxiety.

But don't watch hopelessness from the sidelines. Take a stand against the evil and danger that surround you and your loved ones—fight back! As you begin to take steps of faith, you'll find that there is victory in every situation.

When you understand your authority in Christ Jesus, you will learn how to overcome the enemy's attacks, help loved one's break cycles of bondage and poor decisions, and make your home a place of refuge from spiritual warfare.

This is a time for unity — we should all come into one accord. Together we stand; divided we fall. Trust God's process in your everyday living.

Roundtable Talk

Topic: *God Brought a Thought, From a Throwback*
Scripture Reading:

1. 1 Corinthians 2:10–14
2. Jeremiah 29:11

Taste and See That the Bite Is Worth It

1 Corinthians 2:10–14 (KJV)

10. *But God hath revealed them unto us by his Spirit: for the Spirit searcheth all things, yea, the deep things of God.*

(Some may see themselves in competition with others, but Paul understood that this war is not fought with physical weapons — it is fought with spiritual ones.)

11. *For what man knoweth the things of a man, save the spirit of man which is in him? Even so, the things of God knoweth no man, but the Spirit of God.*

(Paul reminds us that only the Holy Spirit can reveal God's hidden wisdom and divine plan for our lives. We cannot discern these things with our natural senses, but the Spirit of God communes with our spirit and grants prophetic insight — past, present, and future.)

12. *Now we have received, not the spirit of the world, but the Spirit which is of God; that we might know the things that are freely given to us of God.*

(These are God's free gifts to us — words of wisdom, words of knowledge, faith, healing, miracles, prophecy, discernment of spirits, speaking in tongues, and interpretation of tongues.)

13. *Which things also we speak, not in the words which man's wisdom teacheth, but which the Holy Ghost teacheth; comparing spiritual things with spiritual.*

(This verse reminds us to depend completely on the Spirit of God, not on our own wisdom — for He alone is able.)

14. *But the natural man receiveth not the things of the Spirit of God: for they are foolishness unto him; neither can he know them, because they are spiritually discerned.*

(Our unspiritual nature cannot receive the gifts of the Spirit. God's Spirit communicates only with the spirit — divine communion between His Spirit and ours.)

Bible Reflection

The Lord directed His people to leave Babylon because He would bring judgment upon her, and because He would fulfill His promise of Israel's restoration (cf. Jeremiah 51:6; 50:8).

Chapter 3

A PROCESS TO GET TO YOUR PROGRESS

SCRIPTURES ON SPIRITUAL WARFARE — FOR WHEN YOU FACE THE BATTLE

One of the most powerful weapons against the forces of evil is **praying God's Word back to Him**. God's Word reminds us that He knows our path and understands the challenges we face each day.

---

1. Proverbs 14:12

> *"There is a way that seems right to a man, but its end is the way of death."*

2. Isaiah 55:8–9

> *"For my thoughts are not your thoughts, neither are your ways my ways, saith the Lord.*

> *For as the heavens are higher than the earth, so are my ways higher than your ways, and my thoughts than your thoughts."*

These verses remind us that God does not think like humans do. When we encounter obstacles in building His Kingdom, it is often because we rely on our own human solutions — wisdom that is foolish to God. God doesn't need our help; He asks only for **faith** and **obedience**.

Going into Battle

James 4:7 (KJV):

> *"Submit yourselves therefore to God. Resist the devil, and he will flee from you."*

This verse contains **six key elements** to spiritual warfare:

---

1. Submission

Submission to God is a **conscious choice** to follow in Jesus' footsteps and to empty oneself of pride. It is a daily practice of **choosing God's will over your own**, a matter of the heart and mind.

---

2. Resistance

Resistance to the devil is **taking a stand against evil**. It is reminding yourself of God's truth whenever sin or doubt begins to rise in your heart and mind.

3. Spiritual Warfare

Spiritual warfare can only occur when one is **submitted to God** and full of His grace. At this point, Satan is no longer merely attacking you — he is challenging God Himself.

4. Humility

James teaches us to **walk humbly with others**, acknowledging that God alone deserves glory and authority in our lives.

5. Prayer

James 4:6–8 reminds us:

> *"God opposes the proud but gives grace to the humble. Submit yourselves therefore to God. Resist the devil, and he will flee from you. Draw near to God, and He will draw near to you."*

Prayer is essential in submission and resistance. It aligns our heart and spirit with God's will.

A Prayer to Submit to God and Resist the Devil

Heavenly Father,

I bow before You in worship. I submit and surrender myself completely and unreservedly in every area of my life to You, Almighty God.

Your will for me is always my best. Guide my steps, strengthen my faith, and empower me to resist the enemy in all his schemes. Thank You for Your grace, protection, and divine wisdom.

In Jesus' name, Amen.

Chapter 4

HOW TO PRAY AGAINST SPIRITUAL WARFARE ATTACKS

Scripture Foundation: Ephesians 6:10–13 (KJV)

10. *Finally, my brethren, be strong in the Lord, and in the power of his might.*

11. *Put on the whole armour of God, that ye may be able to stand against the wiles of the devil.*

12. *For we wrestle not against flesh and blood, but against principalities, against powers, against the rulers of darkness of this world, against spiritual wickedness in high places.*

13. *Wherefore take unto you the whole armour of God, that ye may be able to withstand in the evil day, and having done all, to stand.*

These verses outline the **seven elements of the whole armour of God**, which equips us to stand firm in spiritual warfare:

The Seven Pieces of the Armour of God

1. Belt of Truth
The belt is buckled around our waist and represents the **truth that comes from the Lord**. It holds everything together and keeps us grounded in God's Word.

2. Breastplate of Righteousness
This protects your **heart against sin** and the enemy's temptations. Living righteously shields your inner life from attacks.

3. Shoes of Peace
The shoes of peace defend against Satan's attacks. They are **gospel-sealed, faith-filled shoes**, enabling us to stand firm in the world while walking in God's Word.

4. Shield of Faith
Faith is our shield. God Himself protects us, and our **faith in Him repels the fiery darts of the enemy**.

5. Helmet of Salvation
The helmet represents **protection of the mind**. It guards our thoughts against deception and spiritual attack.

6. Sword of the Spirit
The Word of God is our spiritual sword, keeping us **rooted, grounded, and prepared for whatever may come our way**.

7. Loins Girt with Truth
Just as Christ is begotten of God, we possess **God's eternal nature within us**, which strengthens and empowers us for every battle.

Bonus: The Shield for Your Back
This completes the full armour of God — **Jesus Christ Himself**. He covers, protects, and strengthens us from all sides.

Prayer Against Spiritual Attacks

O Gracious Father,

We thank You for all You have given and for Your constant presence. We ask forgiveness for our many sins. Thank You for covering and protecting our lives. Strengthen us with Your Spirit and Your Word as we face the challenges of each day. In Jesus' name, Amen.

God's Word: Our Weapon and Guidance

God's will reveal His plan for salvation and new life through the **birth, death, and resurrection of Jesus Christ**. Without God, we can do nothing; with Him, we have purpose, power, and direction.

John 1:1–5 (KJV)

In the beginning was the Word, and the Word was with God, and the Word was God.
The same was in the beginning with God.
All things were made by him; and without him was not anything made that was made.
In him was life; and the life was the light of men.
And the light shineth in darkness; and the darkness comprehended it not.

John 15:7 (KJV)

> *If ye abide in me, and my words abide in you, ye shall ask what ye will, and it shall be done unto you.*

God desires a **relationship with us**, and He has a plan for every life. He is not only God — He is **our Heavenly Father, our protector, and our guide**. Choosing to abide in Him is the key to victory, peace, and purpose.

In ***One Journey to A Final Destiny***, the path of faith is traced as a deeply personal voyage, where every decision, trial, and triumph draws the seeker closer to God's ultimate plan. *Where Do We Go From Here?* takes a complementary perspective, asking the questions that arise when life's certainty fades and guidance is needed—reflecting on God's presence in moments of doubt and transition. Together, these works offer a fuller understanding of faith: one illuminates the journey itself, while the other explores the questions that accompany it, showing that devotion and inquiry are two sides of the same spiritual quest.

Now, we turn to **Dr. Jerome's Perspectives**, where wisdom and experience illuminate the path of faith in ways both practical and profound. Drawing from years of ministry, counseling, and personal reflection, Dr. Jerome offers guidance that bridges the personal journey of *One Journey to A Final Destiny* with the questions posed in *Where Do We Go From Here?*. His insights do not simply answer questions—they invite readers to reflect, grow, and engage with God's presence in every aspect of life. Through his perspective, the threads of both journeys are woven together, revealing a deeper understanding of purpose, devotion, and the spiritual quest that connects us all.

Dr. Jerome D. Brown

The wary hearts and souls of my book *Where Do We Go From Here* reflect my desire to restore peace from God's point of view, based on biblical principles, values, and the Word of God. This work serves as a tribute to the courage and character of all crime victims.

I am an ordained minister of the gospel of Jesus Christ and a certified Christian counselor. I, Dr. Jerome D. Brown, D.N.C., have been a registered student at **Shalom Bible College & Seminary** since August 28, 2005.

I completed a **Bachelor of Divinity** in February 2010, graduating **cum laude**. In June 2011, I earned a **Master's Degree in Theology**, graduating **magna cum laude**. In June 2014, I completed the **Doctoral Program in Nouthetic Counseling (Christian Counseling)**. I am currently enrolled in the **Ph.D. in Philosophy program**, and I am in excellent standing with Shalom Bible College & Seminary of Shalom Ministry in West Des Moines, Iowa.

Shalom Bible College & Seminary is accredited by the **American Accrediting Association of Theological Institutions**, a Christian accreditation association for theological education and religious studies, not a secular accrediting body. I am also a member of **Commence Community Church** in West Des Moines, Iowa.

The **Ph.D. in Philosophy program** is a course of study that focuses on the discussion of theology versus philosophy, incorporating Christian counseling based on the Word of God. I have worked in **prison ministry, Kairos, and various churches**, alongside my late pastor and brother, **Rev. Percy T. Brown Sr.** I have been active in ministry since the age of 12, which has helped me develop empathy for offenders, Christians, and others.

I do not excuse my own offenses or the offenses of others, but I now understand many of the influences that have led to my behavior and that of others. I am able to **condemn sin while recognizing the good** in the hearts and minds of individuals, including myself, even those who are incarcerated.

(See Gen. 24:12–52; Acts 12:5–12; 2 Tim. 2:1–2; Acts 10:1–23; Luke 23:42–43; Hab. 3:1–19; Hab. 1:1–4; 2 Chr. 14:11)

Part 2

Jerome Diego Brown
Where Do We Go from Here?

In our Life Daily encouragement in restoring peace of the basic principles discussed in Jerome D. Brown's book in restoring peace in my life and others are imperative principles as a victim and victims to heal and continue their lives as survivors and not victims. This book will be invaluable tool in communicating these principles and thing happen in my life to anyone dealing with the aftermath of abuse as, Jerome D. Brown uses the threads of loss, anger, hurt, abuse, and dispirit weave a pattern for a life of purpose, self-realization, hope, faith, and love for the collective all of us. Here now is a book that not only gives us insight into how such an approach is applied in a prison setting but-as the subtitle indicates-shows 'Where Do We Go from Here? is not for sissies. It tells of perpetrators who take responsibility for their crimes and victims who face perpetrators and bare their pain and anger. The beauty of this book is that it lays out steps of the spiritual journey for me and us all to take it we want it. Where Do We Go from Here is a marvelous book about how God the Father, Jesus Christ and the Holy Spirit to really restore any broken lives and relationship. Reconciliation and restoration are not easy, but they are very doable if parties will follow the path laid out in the Bible for their lives. I was moved by other people's stories and visions all my life and moved by my story and vision, and my story God told me to tell and given me a vision and since that time at the age of 12 years old as a child I have followed the vision and my life's story is unique as I've drawn upon my own experiences in a groundbreaking disfunction background and my experiences in ministry and prison ministry, has given me a well-written, theologically sound book and a practical method for reconciling our personal relationship and our personal relationship with Jesus Christ God Himself and the Holy Spirit.

<u>**Using Lessons Form My Life Experiences and From Prison to Mend Broken Relationships**</u>

<u>**There can be no better role models of courage, commitment, and unconditional love.**</u>

Acknowledgements

This book, Where Do We Go from Here? is a collaborative effort of restoring peace in others lives as well as mine only through God the Father, Jesus Christ and the Holy Spirit as on our spiritual journey in this life and thereafter to the next life for eternity. The words are mine, but the ideas and spirit are largely from the mind of Christ, and the ideas and spirit are largely from a friend, spiritual daddy Richard James, associative pastor of prison ministry of trinity fellowship church in Amarillo, Texas and my sister Evelyn M. Brown Lee, of Fort Worth, Texas and my friend Linda, of Christs Prison Ministry of O'nell, Ne and Dr. B.L. Rice, of Shalom Bible College of Shalom Ministry and Commerce Community Church by Shalom Ministry INC. of West Des Moines , Iowa, and from others. Therefore, I have many people to acknowledge and thank.

I am working to make this book accurately reflect the concepts and ideas of Where Do We Go from Here and to present them in a way that benefits my family, friends, Christians Men, Christians Women, children's, the young an old alike, sinners and other people's different walks of life, offenders who read my book. Without God the Father, Jesus Christ and the Holy Spirit and Christians men and women mentioned above just to name a few, I have so many people to acknowledge and thank, the book would not have been possible. The real hero of Where

Do We Go From Here of restoring peace the victim- Jesus Christ Himself God's own son and also Christian whom serve Jesus doing the will of God in this life are the victim volunteers themselves- those men and women and children of God have suffered the worst ravages of criminal conduct and yet have chosen to suffer for Jesus Christ and use that suffering to help their fellow human beings who are serving God the Father, Jesus Christ, Holy Spirit and serving time in the United States prison system and foreign country prison system.

All combine to make Where Do We Go from Here, what its s and no doubt all would have graciously contributed to this book in a more direct way had they been asked. All deserve special thanks. Since confidentiality is a critical element of the ministry, I cannot thank them by name and those who were asked and whose stories or contributions I cannot thank them by name, but they know who they are. Thanks for your help.

Several people also made important contributions by providing ideals, discussing issues with me, reading and criticizing drafts of the manuscript, and offering moral and spiritual support. Pastor Richard James and my sister Evelyn Lee and others not mentioned by name agreed to read all or part of the manuscript and keep me as straight as possible on the theological aspects of the Where Do We Go From here experience. I also would very much like to have Pastor Eugene Bank of Fort Worth, Texas, and Pastor James Preston of Fort Worth, Texas and other chaplains to review the manuscript to ensure that it accurately reflects life in the Texas Department of Criminal Justice and in my lifestyle. I like to thank my son, Andrae Jerell Waggoner and my daughter, Clarissa Latrice Dennis, my granddaughter, Nyliah Jordan Wright, their mothers, Charlette Jean Dennise, Doris Waggoner for their input, and suggested innumerable editorial changes that greatly improved the manuscript. Any mistakes that remain are mine alone.

Victim Jerome Diego Brown typically wrote this book 'Where Do We Go from Here" of my experience because I "want to help the offenders" and Christians and sinners and others". Inevitably, However, I Jerome D. Brown quickly learn that it is others who benefit and others receive more than they give. So, it is with me. As a child I thought writing a book would help me and my family and others. I now understand that I am the one receiving the most benefit. Hopefully you will receive some benefit as well. If so, thanks all those acknowledged above.

J.

FOREWORD

This is an edition of Where Do We Go From here that is originally published for the general public in 2026 year. Like my first edition, written on dissertation/ Prison Ministry from Shalom Bible College & Seminary and dissertation/ Child Abuse, it starts Where Do We Go from Here my life started: with Jerome D. Brown, the founder and President and Executive Director of the organization. He is the author of this foreword.

I was enthusiastic back about in 1970-1974 when God first spoke to me when a man of God and women of God Prophesy over my life of the version God has given me to first proposed writing a book about restorative justice process called Where Do We Go from Here, which will be very effectively used in Texas Prisons and elsewhere inside and outside of the United States. I was not certain what shape the book might take or how it would eventually be used, by my inner voice told me that it would be very positive for people lives Where Do We Go from Here. My First edition of the book will be a centerpiece of the Where Do We Go from Here to life curriculum. Thousands or millions or whatever God desire will increase the numbers of copies will be printed and distributed throughout Texas and the world, and I am pleased that

I wrote and authored this edition, not only primarily for incarcerated offenders, but their families, and others outside of prisons.

When I founded Where Do We Go from Here in 2008, I was not aware of the restorative justice movement. I had limited experience in volunteer work inside prisons and preached my first sermon on the Neal unit: Where Do We Go from Here? and has volunteer my time working in the church inside prisons in my 24 years incarcerated since June 4, 1993, but that experience was so powerful that it inspired me to start writing this book called, Where Do We Go from Here in order to make a difference in the lives of crime victims and offenders. At the very core of my passion for this work was the desire to keep other families from going through the years of horror that I and my family experienced after my injustice done to me on June 4, 1993. If this book, Where Do We Go from Here helps incarcerated offenders change their lives and not to commit crimes in the future, then it has prevented innocent families and as myself innocent from being victims of crime.

After experiencing the gut-wrenching aftermath of my incarceration dealing with my racial injustice and injustice by the courts, Texas Prisons System, California State Jail System, For Worth Police Department, Tarrant County Sheriff Department, California Los Angeles Police Department, California Sheriff Department United States Marine Corps, I have great empathy with victims of crime. In my book Where Do We Go from Here, I've defined "Victim" as anyone who has been affected or had a family member or loved one affected by crime, particularly when the incident profoundly changed his or her life, like these events and incidents mentioned herein my book Where Do We Go from here profoundly changed my life. Crime plugs innocent victims as myself into a dark place I did not ask for or deserve. Victims of crime are the very heart and soul of my book Where Do We Go from Here, and I see restoring peace from God's point of view based on biblical principles and values and the word of God as a tribute to the courage and character of all crime victims.

My work as an ordained minister of the Gospel of Jesus Christ and a certified Christian Counselor, Dr. Jerom D. Brown, D.N.C., who has been a registered student at Shalom Bible College & Seminary since August 28, 2005. I have completed a Bachelor of Divinity Degree within February 2010, I completed it with honor, that of Cum Laude, and In June of 2011 I completed a Master Degree in Theology with High Honor, that of Magna Cum Laude, and in June of 2014 I completed the Doctor Program in Nouthetic Counseling (Christian Counseling), and now I am registered at present in their final program, The PH.D. of Philosophy, and I am in excellent standing with Shalom Bible College & Seminary of Shalom Ministry of Wes Des Moines, Iowa is accredited by the American Accrediting Association of Theological Institutions and this is not a secular accreditation; it is a accrediting association for Christian Education and those who are training in religious studies and I am a member of Commerce Community Church of West Des Moines, Iowa, and the Ph. D. of Philosophy Program is a program of study which deals with discussion of Theology Vs. Philosophy, it is a Christian Counseling using the word of God, I have worked In Prison Ministry, Kairos, Churches in Free word, with my deceased Pastor my Brother, Rev. Percy T. Brown, Sr. my brother, Rev. Percy C. Brown, Sr. changed his name to Rev. Percy T. Brown, Sr, and I have worked in the ministry for many years since the age of 12 years old has helped me develop empathy for offenders, Christians and other people's as well. I never excuse my own offenses and others offenses, but I now understand many of the influences that had led to my and others behavior. I am now able to condemn the behavior while recognizing the good that is in the hearts and minds of individuals and myself who are incarcerated (see. Gen. 24:12-52; acts 12:5-12; 1Tim. 2:1,2; Acts 10: 1-33; Luke 23:42, 43; Hab. 3:1-19; 1:1-4; 2Chr. 14:11; Acts 4:24-31; Ezra 9:6-15; 2 King 20:1-11; Rom. 8:26,27; Josh. 7:6-9; Ezra 8:21, 23; Gen. 25:22, 23; Luke 23:34; John 17:1-26; 1King 3:6-14, etc.).

Where Do We Go from Here provides a structure and focus for our reconciliation process that all offenders, Christians and Non-Christians alike can use as a guide to making significant changes in our thinking (see. Ps. 139:23; Isa. 59:7; 1Chr. 28:9; Ps. 139:2; John 5:39; Rom. 12:3; Prov. 23:7; 1Cor. 10;12; 13: 11; Ps. 139:2). The journey to restore peace is much the same for all of us. At our very human core, we have desire for peace ("Shalom") in our lives (Isa. 32:18 see also, Rom. 12:18; Matt. 5:9; James 3:17; Isa.26:3; John 14:27; Gal. 5:22; Col. 3:15 etc.). Life often interrupts or destroys that peace, and we all search for our way back, a return to the peace we knew as a young child or experienced in the good times of our lives. The Journey toward peace requires radical change. It involves a transformation in many of offenders, Christians and Non-Christians alike life process indicate a very significant impact when Jesus Christ changes your heart, mind, and habits (See, Matt. 21:22; Rom. 10:10; Heb. 11:6; 1Tim. 3:2; Jer. 31:33; Phil. 2:5; Jer. 17:9; 24: 7; Ezk. 18:31; 11:19; Ps. 16:17; Jer. 13:23; Acts 10"38; Luke 4:16; Daniel 6:10; etc.).

The principles of Where Do We Go from Here discussed in my book are both simple and complex (see 1King 3:6-14). A "willing heart" is essential to understanding and absorbing this book (see, 1King 3:9-12; Rom. 1:20; Ps. 119:104, 130; 119:34-125; Eph. 1:18; Luke 24:45; Neh. 8:2-13; John 8:43; Isa. 6:9.10; Neb. 11:3; Ex. 31:3, etc.) Read it slowly with an open mind and an open heart. Read the concepts, my story, and adapt them specifically to your life. Let the book 'Speak to you". Our backgrounds and circumstances are so varied that one person's answer is not the same as another person's. One person may need to work on faith, one on forgiveness, and another on repentance, etc. (see, Col. 3:13; Matt. 18:35 2 Cor. 12:13; Rom. 10:17; 2 Thess. 3:2; Heb. 11:1;6:6; 2 Pet. 3:9, etc.). By reading this book, you may be shown some answers about your life that you have never before considered. We should send a great deal of time pondering a quotation from Ernest Hemingway's Farewell to arms; "The world breaks everyone, and afterwards, some are strong at the broken places". (See. Mark 5:1-43 Ps. 51:1-19; 52:1-9; Acts 3:1-26; 2Tim. 1:15: Rev. 2,3; Acts 9:1-22, etc.) A significant part of my journey after I went to prison. My granddaughter Nyliah Jordan Wright was born in 2016 was toward becoming strong where I had been broken (see, Luke 22:32; 2Tim. 4:17; Rom. 15:1; 2 Cor. 12:10; 2 Sam

11:1-27; 12:1-23 etc.) For a number of years, that seemed impossible (See Luke 1:37; Heb. 11:6). I continued to feel broken by my first ex-wife's Gena R. Daniels Brown miscarriage of the baby, and when I came back to Texas of another ex-girlfriend Mechall D. Pattersons miscarriage of the twin boys, and me wind up in prisoned and other difficulties and hardships that life presented me. I continued to seek the path toward restoring my inner peace and eventually, it led me to write this book Where Do We Go from Here. I believe that all who continue to seek will find their way to peace. It takes work, patience and persistence; and this book can be an important part of your journey toward becoming "Strong at the broken places" (See Ps. 147:3; Isa. 53:5; James 1:3, 4; Luke 11:8; etc.).

I hope and pray that when you read this book that it was a major step for you toward restoring peace in your lives. I am grateful to the many employees of the Texas Prison System who helm me offenders and my family along the way who help me implement this book and others who worked with passion, persistence, and focus to help me complete the first edition of Where Do We Go from Here and to make the changes resulting in this edition.

As a final comment, I request of you, don't make lasting judgments or decisions as to what effect it had on you until you have finished the book Where Do We Go from Here. This is a total process that must be completed to have significant and lasting effect.

I pray that this book and will be a blessing for you and your family. I applaud you for participating and complete the book and any other programs that you may participating give it your best effort.

JJ.

Introduction

In May 31, 1964, Jerome Diego Brown was born to a Christian family in Fort Worth, Texas, at John Peter Smith Hospital, his father, J. B. Brown, Sr. he was born in Marshall, Texas and my mother was, Willie Dean Hayes Brown, she was born in Houston, Texas. I had 20 brothers and five sisters, this what I was told when I was a child growing up in Fort Worth, Texas. We went to church on a regular basic an at the age of 12 years old under the leadership of Rev. Chase I became a Christian giving my life to Christ Jesus, through our family too poor as I though as I found out later on during my sentenced term my father, J. B. Brown, Sr. and my mother Willie Dean Brown had land in Marshall Texas on the site off East Texas Baptist University as my oldest brother Jerry W. Brown changed his name to J. B. Brown, Jr. advised me that my other brothers and sisters got paid of their of the land, and God appears to me in a dream and told me don't sell the land. In about 1968 through 1974 I attended Carl Peak Elementary and Diamond Hill Elementary Schools in Fort Worth, Texas. In about 1973 when I attended Diamond Hill Elementary School, I was struck on the forehead with a baseball bat and rushed to the emergency room at John Peter Smith Hospital when I was born at, and while attending Carl Park Elementary School I was born at, and while attending Carl Park Elementary School I claimed over a wired fence and cut my left hand open and had to be rushed again to the emergency room at that same hospital location for some stitched. And at home I were playing with my dog and pulled his tail while the dog was eating and the dog bit my nose almost off and I had to be rushed to the emergency room again. When I was born, I had to stay in the hospital for about three months and I like to died because I had a massive lump in my neck cutting of my breathing, I were losing weight fast and dying because I were premature. All the Christians, friends and church members overcome with grief, went in prayer asking God for a miracle to spare my life resulting in me living, Jerome D. Brown at the age of 12 years old resolved to devote the rest of his life to the service of God and the poor and others. About the age of 13 years of age I was struck by a Fort Worth Police Car, unfortunately, as a child I were going from the store to home riding my bike and all of sudden I was hit by a police car, almost resulting in my own death of which the Fort Worth Police Department cover the incident up in the community.

That after this incident with the Police Department Fort Worth our family decided to move to Los Angeles California to live with my oldest brother, Rev. Percy C. Brown, Sr. and his girlfriend, Mrs. Ann Arrainton and later on my brothers Michael G. E. Brown, Darryl Glenn Brown, Willie Dean Brown II, came up to California to live and my mother Willie Dean Brown I came this was in early 1974. All while I were up in California I always get into fights and other individuals committing violent crimes against me, as I tried in life truly to help those with trouble in their lives to turn themselves around, but of course, turn on me in school. Throughout my school years living in California, I had to walk to school to attend Raph Burnch Elementary where I were beat up and at that time I met two good friend's young boys, Mickey Lust and K. C. Porter whom taught me how to fight back and when I did fight back I went back to home and got a base ball bat and brought it to school and began hitting those young boys on the play ground in front of their friends and their girlfriends who became good friends with me and my friends, and when I went home these young boys I did not know were in gangs and those girls whom came to my house ands surrounded the apartment complex and my brother Rev. Brown had to call the police and later on we moved away to somewhere else. I never wanted to go to California because I knew it meant trouble for me and new violent crimes was going to happen to me. I were in prison in my own brother's home, I come form a dysfunctional or broken home I was always lied on and beat and later raped by my oldest brother whom are deceased Ray Brown, he always takes me everywhere with him and molest me and my other brothers and sisters given me drugs and alcohol and used it excessive consumption of and psychophysiological dependence on alcoholic beverages at age 12 years old. At the age of 13 years old an old lady had me to have sex with her and my sister Willie Dean Brown walked in the room and caught us and told our mother, and I was beaten for that behavior and my actions when I was tied across the bed and beaten naked and that made me afraid, hurt, angry- and I want to run away and I did to Pastor Earl Harper house and told them what happen of all my abuse in that house. I never knew my father, my mother, brothers, sisters, and relatives' event though I lived with them. I heard my father whom I never knew abused my mother, his children's and that's why I've been abused and abusively to others. My family members used drugs and often sell them to others. Some of my family members themselves in prison, dead, or even in jail. You want to turn your life around, but you don't know how. This book is for all of you.

When I lived at 1717 E. Harvey Street in Fort Worth, Texas, I was locked in a room without lights at times and sometimes afraid of the dark but I find myself talking to God about what I were going through as a child about my abuse in this home when the mother I never knew had to go to work and I always wonder what would happen next to me. I wanted to commit suicide at a young at about 8 years old because I had not finally come to understand something that I had not seen or experienced before. As I write this book, I finally understood that young boys and girls who are locked up in youth faculties are very often just stopping over in their way to the big house- to an adult prison.

And we also understood that you-offending youth and adults alike- nearly always have much in common. With a few exceptions, you come from a dysfunctional or broken home. Perhaps you never knew your father and your mother deserted you. Or your father, you abused your children-and you. Or your parents used drugs and often sell them to others. Or your mother is a prostitute, or one or both of your parents are themselves in jail or prison or dead. And you are afraid, hurt, angry-and you want to get even. You skipped out on school and used alcohol and drugs when you knew better or you did not know better. You joined a gang so you would have a "family". Or you did some shoplifting-or maybe sold some drugs, or perhaps committed burglary-to get what you want. You lashed out and hurt others- maybe even physically attacked them or murdered them. You got caught. You want to turn your life around, but you don't know how. This book Where Do We Go from here is for all of you.

It's important to remember that you and I need to be concerned with our behavior, and not with our value as a person or our worth as one of God's children. Back in California I were continuedly beaten and placed in a drared room without lights and a T.U. turned on remained in that room doing housework, homework, while my brothers and sisters were having fun and had met to their lessons sometimes, and in this way, I can go outside and sometimes watch T.V. and even eat with the family and not in my room, and get ready for church, but the physical abuse did not stop not taking advantage of me when I received my SSI income checks I did not receive until I was evidently in the 121th grade to graduated at the age of 22 years of age because I was in a special education classes and I almost committed suicide in high school and transferred to Centennial High School and graduate. And attempted to go to Compton Community Junior College, and attempted to go to Los Angeles Southwest College, and went to Long Beach College of business. In 1983, after I graduated from Centennial Sr. High School in California, the lady whom raised me as I heard stories about her (Ms. Willie Dean Brown I.) was my grandmother and her daughter Q.T. Brown was my real mother because she had to give me to her mother-Ms. Brown because she was too young at the age about 12 years old when she had her first child. And this brought on confecting stories about my birth in question of my personal fears or concerns on how to approach this matter, but since I have Jesus in my life and heart. I can approach it not feeling responsible about something that isn't my fault about my birth, and when Ms. Brown died of and heart attack and stroke in California, I was working at Chucke Cheese in Carson Mall in Carson, California and my supervisor was a Pastor George, whom let me off work that day and telling me to come back when ever I feel like coming back to work because he knew my brother Rev. Brown where a pastor, but did not know about my abuse from my family and Rev. Brown as I kept it hidden from other peoples and not God cause I talked to God in the dark as I were raise that way in the darkrooms.

In 1984-1985 I enlisted in the United Staes Marines Corps at basic training at San Diego, California during that time period I acquired psychiatric, disorder claimed as mental illness and post traumatic stress disorder ("PTSD") and my claim for service connection for PTSD from a personal assault. In April 2009 and In June 4, 1993, after the illegally arrest, I informed the VA (Veterans Affairs) and my trial attorney, Larry M. Moore that I had been illegally discharged from the USMC and that I was abused, harassed, threatened and subject to discrimination because I reported my drill instructor to the proper authorities after the drill instructor violated someone else's rights. PTSD is by definition a mental illness. I raised my issues of personal assault causing me PTSD within my letters to the VA and informed my trial counsel, Mr. Moore and my VA requests for release information for my mental illness claim. I explain the actions that led to my PTSD claim based on personal assault, which is the indictments causing his mental illness. I state the basis of my mental illness claim in a letter on August 7, 2010. I says that the drill instructor sergeant I witnessed assaulting another individual, the basis of his mental illness, threatened to kill him and "took off his hat, belt, and shirt and took and offensive stand towards me and out me in fear grave fear (SIC) for my own life and safety". I further state the USMC "caused the harm to me during basic training at San Diego and did conspire to harm me physically". These events constitute my PTSD claim based on personal assault, which have been entwined with my mental illness claim. The board of Veterans Appeals and mental health professionals acknowledged that as a veteran and an offender prisoner of State of Texas and my history of background I have been diagnosed with a number of psychiatric conditions. The board of veterans appeals also acknowledged that Mr. Brown the Veteran's Personnel Records shows that he committed a number of breaches of military discipline for which he was counselled and given non-judicial punishment. The board further acknowledged that Mr. Brown was subsequently found 'unable to adapt to military environment and was given an administrative entry level separation from service on account of his performance and conduct". Furthermore, Mr. Brown has described two and others separate in service events and two separate outside of prison events that have caused him mental illness and his raped as a child by his oldest deceased, brother Ray Brown and his family knew about these incidents events and kept them hidden and also child protective health and human services, social security services and I am partly sure the criminal district attorney office and Fort Worth Police Department and Local Law Enforcements officials and that my own trial counsel, Larry M. Moore knows about that I've told him about all these situations, my family and friends as well. The veteran (Mr. Brown) inability "to adapt to the military environment" could have been caused by the assaults and threats- but there is insufficient evidence to make this determination because the military had no medical examination was conducted.

In 1992-1993 before my incarceration, I attend this church, church of God in Christ of Fort Worth, Texas, Pastored by Rev. James Preston where Rev. Preston allowed me to preach and to evangelize and salvation to others by faith in Christ (see. 1 Cor. 16:13 Rom. 10:14,15, etc.). Some churches excepted me and some rejected me only because of Christ. The topic of my sermon was: "Have Faith in God Little Children" (see Heb. 11:1). At that time when I allowed the holy spirit power to work through me, sudden in the middle of sermon, I saw Jesus Christ himself appeared to me as I stopped Jesus kept on coming towards me and stopped and I stopped right in the sermon when my pastor's wife was sitting in the front row seat looking directly at me and as I heard the heavenly choir singing: The song was – 'Telling Peoples to come to Jesus just now". I gave the invitation and thereafter I felled sick, had a stroke, and had to be rushed to the hospital when I stayed in the hospital for about two or three weeks, when my son, Andrae Jerell Waggoner and his mother Doris Faye Waggoner and other peoples came in the hospital to see me and where I worked at John Peter Smith Hospital in Fort Worth, Texas, whom later on my co-workers and supervisors set me up to get me fired saying I wasn't doing my job in which this was a lie. I was up for promotion as supervisor and the word got back to me and my co-worker conspired with the supervisor to lie to get me fired. I did not reveal anything to the church or others until later on to my sister, Evely M. Brown Lee and other Christians, as I talked to my sister Ms. Lee over the telephone at the Nathaniel J. Neal unit in Amarillo, Texas and she did not believe me and told me no one has seen God and lived. In 1992. I worked at John Peter Smith Hospital in Fort Worth as a house keeper and one day the Holy Spirit led me to go to ICU upstairs where this family was in the waiting room and I asked the nurse where is he and she told me he's in the room asleep. God instructed me to tell the nurse do not let no one in the room. I went into the room and took out my praying oil and the holy spirit told me that death is in his foots and I was instructed to anoint the room, his bed and body and shake his foots and command death to leave him and told him you shall live and not die! And I let the room and went out to the waiting room and told the family and a little girl that he be out of the hospital in three days. On the 3rd day, I was off work and I went in and I was moping the floor and when I looked up there, they were coming out of the elevator with him and that little girl and their family praising God and giving him thanks for God using me on that day.

In 1992-1993, before my incarceration I was staying with a friend his name is Russell because my son mother, Doris Faye Waggoner had kicked me out her apartment because I did not want to marry her and I am waiting on my wife from God (see Proverbs 31:1-31), and not to do it my own way like before I got married in California and it was a mess and reck. As I was trying to find employment of which she thought I was not seeking a job. After moving in with my friend Russell I received a telephone call to come to Doris's apartment quickly due to my son Andrae were ill and his fever was 101-102. I told my son mother, Doris, the devil are in this house and death, open all the windows and doors and the Holy Spirit instructed me to take my son, Andrae into the other room and close the door behind me and do not let no one in the room also run cold water in the bathtub and rub praying oil all over his body and baptized him in Jesus Name, and the father and God and of the Holy Spirit , and after the fever broke and he was running around and she asked me what happened and why she couldn't do it then as I explained things to her, what God told me to do to him.

In 1991-1992, during this period of time I was over to ex-girlfriend mother's apartment, Ms. Dian Woodly, of whom my ex-girlfriend, T. Woodly and when I arrived to the apartment, I did not notice several objects of Red Dolls and lights of small candles all over this apartment in each room. As I came inside the apartment and sat down on a couch for a few minutes and afterward went into the bed room to have intercourse with her, and while we were having intercourse as I went inside her, I notice of her face expression changed, her eyes were black and darked, her skin changed to dark and then a voice came out of her, "saying we I got want I wanted". When I injected my sperm inside of her. Then me and her started fighting and I grabbed the anointing oil and poured the bottle of oil down her mouth and pleaded the blood of Jesus over her and me because I knew just what happen the evil spirits and the devil were inside of that apartment complex and the apartment. Then the Holy Spirit had me going throughout that apartment blowing out those candles and pulling off the devil dolls head pleading the blood of Jesus in that apartment and that apartment complex. When this incident was over with, I asked my ex-girlfriend, T. Woodly and her so-called cousin of which both my ex-girlfriend, T. Woodly and her relative where lesbians sleeping with each other as I found this out later on in a dispute and argument between us because my relative had sex relation with my ex-girlfriend, I did not know this man were my relative until I got incarcerated in June 4, 1993 incident. They said they did not know what had happen. I did not know until the Holy Spiri revealed what had just taken place because my ex-girlfriend, T. Woodly her father-in-law was taking his two little children's age 7 and 9 years of old, her mother and my ex-girlfriend, T. Woodly, Diana Woodly to devil worshiper-services, and later on after I found out that the father-in-law was going around molesting his own children. Other children and my ex-girlfriend and raping them every where the lived at in the community and the district attorney Tim Curry and other city officials did nothing to stop it.

In June 4, 1993, incident before my incarceration telling this part of my story is difficult and heartbreaking, because it forced me to relive in great detail that horrible night. But it also gave me a powerful sense of release, as if my facing my ordeal I was able to take the first step toward letting go of it. I, Jerome D. Brown still suffers daily from the tragedy of the horrible night of those girls above unnamed and named mentioned in my story Where Do We Go from Here when I stabbed my ex-father-in-law with a knife, for the things he done to those girls and others and stolen my things and did things to me and got me them on drugs. These girls never had a chance of an unspeakable horrors of the starting point for me been set free on the inside in my heart and for that family too. In 1993, Jerome D. Brown I was in jail I called my Pastor James Preston, when I received that terrible phone call on the other end on the line that morning or evening, 1993, from my Pastor James Preston, Church of God in Christ in Fort Worth, Texas. My Pastor, James Preston, said, "Son, did you have any drug on you? I said no pastor, you don't believe me I preached in your church and told you all about me and where I go and do and you don't believe me? My Pastor, James Preston said, the police said you had drugs on you, and my Pastor James Preston said he tried to have a pastor that is a superintendent and church people to help me to call my old friend Pastor Eugene Ranks who tricked me out of my money $3, 500 after I signed my check to him after he said Pastor Ranks were going to help me out to marry me and get me an apartment with my ex-girlfriend T. Woodly which was a lied to me. I filed suit against Pastor Bank and later on dismissed the state lawsuit because after praying and talking to God and other Christians about the matters what I was going through I finally forgave him and moved o with my life and ministry. My Pastor James Preston, told me something horrible has happened. Diane Woodly's dead! Someone has robbed her and killed her!" I did not ask questions, but I told my Pastor James Preston, I know that her ex-boyfriend did it but I can't prove it because of what I have done to him, Diana Woodly never had a chance.

In 1993, where I was living with my friend Russell and at that time another friend spent the night several times at Russell's apartment and his name is unknown of which he is a minister of the Gospel of Jesus Christ whom were dealing with his health problems of AIDS HIV as I accepted him not matter what's was wrong with him, but of course, I had to confront his pastor about the mistreatment of the minister of his church whom have AIDS HIV accordingly to the Word of God in Faith, Love, Mercy, no matter what the outcome of this situation was it had anger me in my spirit and grieved the holy spirit based on the word of God (see for example 2 King 19:14-19; 20-37, 20:1-11: 1Thess. 5:19: Matt. 8:14, 15; Lk. 16:20, etc.) The minister asked me to go with him to a friend that's dying with AID HIV at this apartment whom I was met with the dying mother and the son in the back bedroom at the apartment when I walked in, I smelled a bad odor in the apartment and sitting on a couch in the front living room were about four guys, there where homosexual and the other one a very young not an homosexual because the others where trying to have this young man to engage In homosexual conduct, when the Holy Spirit laid my eyes on this young man before I entered the dying death bedroom with his grieving mother. As I listen to the mother and tried my best to acknowledge the dying my full attention. I only asked one or two questions; One question was: Are he saved? And I can't remember the other one. "While he was dying, I led him to Christ Jesus, and I saw two angels, death angels came and leave and suddenly the heavenly angels came and took him away in peace, and the mother saw them and she believed, and I heard the heavenly choir sang "Telling and singing the song, "come to Jesus just now". Before I left that apartment the Lord led me to tell these for young men to accept Jesus as their Lord and savior and believe the gospel. These young men were about 17 to 21 years old in the living room. The spirit of God told me to tell them this is your last chance to com to Jesus or death shall be your reward, only one came to Jesus, the young man, but the others rejected Jesus and I left with this young man and we are drove to his mother home and he repented and we were saved (see Acts 5:14; 1Tim. 4:12; Acts 2:40; 16:30, etc.).

In 1992-1993 I were living with a relative whom I never truly knew was this my mother or sister, Q.T. Brown as far as I was told throughout my lifetime, I lived with Q.T. Brown off and on, and with whom also I was told she was my mother or grandmother, Willie Dean Hayes Brown, I, her daughter is Q.T. Brown until I found out the hidden mystery of the family's secret, I must continue on my journey towards the truth function matters until God through the Holy Spirit reveal it to me; and thus, God led me to tell my niece, Romona L. Brown, this Q.T. Brown's daughter, her brother Myron Brown that he was not going to see the year 1993, when Myron Brown started a fight with me and then I told Myron Brown I forgave you, you are my real brother not your uncle. One night about in 1992-1993 before 1993 I were living in Hulen Area in Fort Worth on the west side of town and I received a telephone call from my oldest sister, Evelyn M. Brown Lee's daughter, Yvette Brown, she's married now Yvette Brown Green whom also I also thought my sister, Evelyn M. Brown Lee whether she's my sister or aunt or not, Yvette Green, phoned me later that night at approximately 10:00 PM, about in 1992-1993, she said, Myron's dead! I remember telling Myron that he would die and not see 1993 year. That year between 1992-1993 my niece, Yvette Green called channel eight news team in Dallas-Fort Worth area prompted them to investigate Myron's murder and Myron's murderers were arrested within forty-eight hours. The Dallas Channel Eight News Team in Dallas-Fort Worth area investigated and found out that it was a conspiracy to commit murder against Myron

Brown and several about nineteen year old had been at a night club in Fort Worth neighborhood that night drinking, partying with friends and Myron Brown's girlfriend whom was not arrested but part of the investigations conducted by the Dallas Channel Eight News Team and Fort Worth District Attorney's Office, Tim Curry, Criminal District Attorney whom later on brought indictments and criminal charges against those individuals for Myron Brown's murder. Romana Brown's ex-boyfriend, her daughter's father, my ex-brother-in-law had given a handgun to a about the age nineteen-year-old and fired the fatal shot in either the right or left side behind the ear and the bullet pincered an artery and came off out his side where he bullet came out as I was told and my family by the funeral director, we knew of a long-time friend who later were murdered by his gay friends setting Dr. Gregory Spencer of Fort Worth, Texas, and were a Pastor of the Philadelphia Church of Fort Worth, Texas, Dr. Gregory Spencer picks up young men in exchange for sexual favors of money, clothes, etc. And so that the reasons why these young several about nineteen-years old murdered him, tied him up with duct tape and cut off his penis and placed his penis in his mouth and cut his throat, Dr. Spencer's murderers were arrested and this information came from individuals and news articles that these individuals were at the funeral. I did tell Romona Brown what was going to happen as the Holy Spirit revealed it to me and I told her to get rid of her ex-boyfriend whom were going to set Myron Brown up to be killed, Roma Brown did not believe me, and when did happen I was ministering a lady out of town. When God gave me the vision of the incident as to what actual taken place, and afterward I told the lady over the phone I call her back, but I did not reveal to the lady over the phone nor my family and my relative, Yvette Green called me and told me what had just happen to Myron Brown is dead and I remember as to what God had told me about this incident occurred (see, Joel 2:28; 1 Cor. 13: 9; Matt. 10:41, 13:57; John 6:14; Acts 11:5, 26:19; Col. 1:28; Titus 3:11, etc.).

In 1980, I lived at 124th Street Los Angeles, California, where I attended Centennial Sr. High School in the 10th grade, my oldest brother, Darryl

Glenn Brown and niece Katie Maye Brown Barns because she got married, when I use to walk to school and I had a friend across the street from were I lived with my oldest brother, Rev. Brown and his wife, Ella C. Brown and my sick mother, Willie Dean Brown I at that time of me living there and going to school on that particular day I decide to over to my friend's house because I notice It as sometimes dark and he did not come out of his house only a few times, this day at evening at approximately 3:00 PM I went over and knocked on the front door and he invited me inside so me been looking around the house and I pepped into his mother's room and I noticed a small box with little doors open up and it does and small dolls all around this box and candles light up all over the room, so I decided to leave and surprise when I begin to close her bedroom door she was behind me and an evil spirit gripped me and suddenly his mother told me she not going to hurt me but I only want your soul, my friend stood still and I opened the front door and left out and ran across the street fast as I could and I did not tell nobody what had happened to me and what was going on in that house because I did not know what to do and how to explain it and trust anybody. I just talked to God in the dark room all alone when I was by my self and I walked around the other way going to school in fear and knowing something was wrong and the devil was real. (See, 1 Sam. 15:23; Kin. 9:22;2Chr. 33:6; 1Sam. 28:3,9; Deut. 18:9-14 etc.).

In 1987-1989, I was living with my oldest brother Rev. Bown at 2131 San Vincente Compton, California with my ex-wife, Gena R. Daniel Brown of which my brother, Rev. Brown did not want me to get married nor marry this lady as I did end up marrying her but later on filed for a divorce my spiritual father Rev. Earl Green in Los Angeles, California od AML Church Los Angeles California filed the paperwork because Gena was already married at that time, when I were living there with my brother, Rev. Brown he kept it very hot inside his house in the summer time when we both saw my brother Rev. Brown chatting over us and I was hoping and moving all around. And on another day my ex-wife Gena and I had the same dream when I saw several young boys running away from this dead body and the dead body did not have any clothes on and God appeared to me in that dream and told me don't sell the land and that's when my ex-wife Gena confronted my brother Rev. Brown concerning the dream and the deeds to the land because he and them in his desk draw. On another day in the morning, I went to talk to my brother's wife, Ella whom were telling me that I don't know about my birth that's something is wrong with my birth and about the time she was going to tell me my brother Rev. Brown walked into the room and she kept quiet. On another day, I was trying to have sex with my ex-wife Gena and she keep on telling me no, but I did it anyway and when I went to have sex with her, she was bleeding cleaning herself and I thought it was alright to have sex while a woman going through her cleaning period of her body because I didn't understand this God taught me a valuable lesson to learn and to pass on to others. So, this what happen to me as I went to sleep I the bedroom my spirit left my body and now my spirit is over my body in the bed looking down at it, and then my body when straight to hell while I were in hello I saw doors, peoples in hell and they were screaming, the doors were round and I walked through that door and I did not want to be there so I call on Jesus in my thoughts. And sudden my spirit went upward into heaven where I saw the gates and I looked inside over the gates and saw clear streets and golden floors and I heard a voice and it said its not time and I went back into my body and when that happen, I heard the foot steps of God in the cool of that evening day and I hid myself because I were scared to death and I went to my ex-wife Gena and asked her to forgive me and I promised I wouldn't do that again. I don't know how long I was in hell or heaven maybe one minute.

Remember when the word hell used to be considered a curse word? We must never repeat what we learned from our neighborhood boys and girls and others and got our tongue swabbed with a bar of soap or something-just for saying hell. Oh, how times have changed! These days the words have permitted our culture. Hell is hardly considered a curse word or even a "bad" word, and it has steadily become part of our cultural slang, a figure of speech that has erupt into our everyday vocabulary. Television and movies have inundated us with the use of the word so that we have hardly notice when its being used. How many times have you or me heard a character say, "Go to Hell" or "hell, no!" or someone casually use a phrase like "hot as hell", in everyday discussions?

Since the significance of the word has been culturally watered down, it would be reassuring to find the true definition, impact, and consequences of hell preached from our nation's pulpits. But the hell fire and brimstone message of Dante's inferno a popular subject years ago in various denominations is no longer a popular subject with modern-day "Religiously correct" churches. In fact, hell is considered "too negative" for most preachers, who are afraid of scaring away their growing congregations. The idea that a person could actually spend eternity in hell seems to have been deleted from the church, along with moral absolutes.

Although America is generally considered a Christian Nation, in fact, there are a large number of people who are non-Christian or practice no religion at all. A recent poll asked more than a thousand Americans about the subject of eternal life, and 67 percent believed that their souls would go to heaven or hell when they died, while 24 percent did not believe that either heaven or hell even existed. That statistic-the people who don't believe heaven or hell exists-is why I'm passionate about sharing my own story and writing this book, "Where do we Go from Here". God has sent Jerome D. Brown with a wake-up message for you and those you love, because God doesn't want anyone to spend eternity without him. Hell is a real place and heaven, but telling people they might go there is not an easy or popular message. God knew what he was doing when he gave Jerome Brown the difficult task of sharing his story. He knew Jerome D. Brown's character, his integrity, his faith, his love, his family, his friends and his ex-wife, his godly children, his mother, who supports him with their amazing prayers would guard the message with truth and protect it with honor. I am privileged to be a part of this extraordinary gift from God.

"They shall go down to the bars of the Pit" (see, Job 17:16, KJV); "The Earth with her bars was about me forever: yet hast thou brought up my life from corruption" (See, Jon. 2:6, KJV). "For a fire is kindled in my anger, and shall burn to the lowest hell' (see, Deut. 32:22); "… Suffering the vengeance of eternal fire" (see, Jude 7).

I was horrified as I heard the screams of an untold multitude of people crying out in torment. It was absolutely deafening. The terror-filled screams seemed to go right through me, penetrating my very being. I once heard about a television special where a news reporter spent the night in a prison just to experience prison life firsthand. The prisoners were crying, moaning, and yelling all night long. He stated that he couldn't sleep because of all the noise. This place where I now stood was far, far worse.

Through the panic and the deafening noise, I struggled to gather my thoughts. I'm in hell! This is a real place, and I'm actually here! I frantically tried to understand, but it was just so inconceivable. Not me, I'm a good person, I thought. The fear was so intense I couldn't bear it, but again, I couldn't die. I knew that most people upon the surface of the earth did not believe or even know that there was a whole word going on down here. They wouldn't believe it. But here it existed, and it was all too real. This place was so terrifying, so intense, and so hostile that it would be impossible to me to exaggerate the horror. I did not know how I had arrived there. The fact that I knew God was kept from my mind. This was explained to me later by the Lord himself and through prison and events in my life experiences. In retrospect, I knew that there are several scriptures indicating that God does sometimes hide things from man's or women's mind (see LK. 18:34 Daniel 4:34). As I stood outside the door, I actually felt the darkness and when I went to hell. Exodus 10:21 speaks of "… Darkness which may even be felt". It was not like the darkness on the earth. It was as though the darkness had its own power, a power that consumed me (see Lk. 22:53; 2 Pet. 2:17; Prov. 20:20; Jude 13). The darkness was not simply the absence of light- it had a distinctive evil presence, a feeling of death, a penetrating evil.

Some scientists have reported that the core temperature at the center of the earth is approximately twelve thousand degrees. To endure that for an eternity is unfathomable. There is in hello is no safe place, no safe moment, no temporary relief of any kind (see Prov. 1:33). In some cases, their victims knew death would come by brutal decapitation. Try to imagine the terror these victims must have felt as they awaited their fate. In hell, this state of fear never ceases for even one second. It lasts for an eternity.

I remember, as a child, stepping into several fights to protect kids who were weaker and who were being bullied. I was broken up several times, but I couldn't just stand there and not help. The television actors who enforced justice and guarded the weak were my role models. To look out for others is a godly characteristic. Since we all come from God it is in most people to feel this way. We have seen how our country always comes to the rescue for the rest of the world. This inborn desire to protect the defenseless continued in my adult life. Now, without the ability to help even one defenseless, tormented soul, I felt the hopelessness unending torment was more that I could bear. Now try to picture the most fearful moment of your life (See Erwin Lutzer, one minute after you die (Chicago: Moody Publishers, 1997), 112; Ps. 11:6-7; 1Cor. 10:10; Ps. 140:10; Job 16:6; Thomas Vincent, Fire and Brimstone (Morgan, Pa: 26:6; Soli Deo Gloria Publications, 1999), 111-112).

<u>What you believe it important</u>

Why should you believe me?

I can appreciate and understand why you might be skeptical in regard to my experience. I know I would be. I came from a conservative background where I received sound biblical teaching from conservative bible teachers who would probably shown my experience. These learned Ph. D's and college professors would agree that hell exists and would not have a problem with most of the scriptures contained in my book Where Do We Go from here and in appendix A.

However, it is very likely that many of them would have an incredulous opinion about God taking someone there for an experience such as the one I had. And I would agree, for I to have been skeptical of such "experiences" in the past. Yet the fact remains that this did occur to me, and scripture supports that such an experience could take place.

In looking back, it took nearly years ago for meto settle down from the effects of this experience and other experiences. A bad dream or even a nightmare would not nearly have the same effect on someone. I was completely traumatized after the return and other experiences and now prison, and only the Lord, through the prayers of my family, my children's, Christians and others, brought me out of it. My life will never be the same in how I view anyone who does not know him. I will do all I can to share the truth with others.

If you choose not to believe me, it really doesn't matter. It is not my experience that is important for you to believe, but what the word of God has to day about the matter. I sincerely hope my experience will cause you to investigate the scriptures for yourself.

<u>Why should you believe the bible?</u>

Many people go through life never taking the time to investigate what the bible has to say. Some think it Is simply a collection of quaint stories and colorful metaphors. Others will say, "It is a good history book but has no relevance to my life". Still others believe it is written for people who, in the past, were simple minded, or they believe that the bible is no longer relevant in our modern society.

People will usually believe whatever religious beliefs they were raised with and not question them. They adhere to that old saying, "Never discuss religion or politics, "thereby remaining uninformed on the subject. It is not my intent to disparage another's beliefs, but rather to extend to them facts to which they may not have had exposure. Dr. Chuck Missler said, "One of the penalties of our casual or reluctant attitude about death and dying is that most people are steeped in myths and misconceptions. Almost every commonly held belief is erroneous, misleading and contrary to what we do know about the subject.

Dr. Robert Dick Wilson said, "I have made it an invariable habit never to accept an objection to a statement of the Old Testament without subjecting it to a most through investigation, linguistically and factually. He holds a Ph. D. from Princeton and is author of a scientific investigation of the Old Testament.

Many of the founding fathers of this great country believed in the absolute truth of God's word. Here is a sampling of their comments:

You do well to wish to learn our arts and way of life, and above all, the religion of Jesus Christ... Congress will do everything they can to assist you in this wise intention. – George Washington

The first and almost the only book deserved of universal attention is the Bible – John Quincy Adams

Does God use dreams and visions?

I have had several dreams from the Lord in regard to the bible. Even in very realistic dreams, they are not analogous to an actual visit to hell. Job said, "Then you scare me with dreams and terrify me with visions (See, Job 7:14; 2Cor. 12:1-2; Acts 7:56; Rev. 1:10; Acts 9:3-4).

Erwin W. Lutzer, who has graduate degree from Dallas Theological Seminary, Loyola University, and Simon Greenleaf School of Law, said, "If Stephen saw our Lord before he died, and if Paul died and was caught up into paradise, it is just possible that others believers might also have such a vision… we should not expect such experiences, but they could happen.

Habakkuk 2:2 states: "Then the Lord answered me and said: "Write the vision and make it plain".

The bible is not just "A" book, but a collection of sixty-six books written by at least forty authors over approximately a fifteen-hundred-year period. The authors were historians, military, generals, prophets, kings, politicians, a doctor, a rabbi, fishermen and even a tax collector. It was written on three continents and in three different languages: Hebrew, Greek, and Aramaic (See, Josh Medowell, evidence that demands a verdict, Nashville, TN: Nelson reference 1999), 15-17). They all wrote about the coming savior. Every word that inspired by God. (See 2Tim. 3:16). The famous poet Voltaire said that within one hundred years of his time, Christianity would be "swept from existence and passed into history". Yet fifty years after his death, the Geneva Bible Society used his house and printing press to produce stacks of bibles (see, McDowell, evidence that demands a verdict, 20). Jesus himself made this statement: "… my words will by no means pass away" (see, Mark 13:31). Dr. H.L. Hastings, a well-known writer, is cited saying, "If this book had not been the book of God, men would have destroyed it long ago. Emperors, and popes, kings and priests, princess and rulers have all tried their hand at it; they die and the book still lives. (Ibid., 21). There are more than three hundred prophecies in the Old Testament in regard to the birth, life, death and resurrection of Jesus.

No other book has been written foretelling the future with such accuracy. Professor Wilber Smith, DD, who taught at Fuller Theological Seminary and Trinity Evangelical Divinity School, said, "Not in the entire gamut of Greek and Latin Literature… can we find any real specific prophecy of a great historic event to come in the distant future, nor any prophecy pf a savior arises in the human race… neither can the founders of any cult in this country rightly identify and ancient text specifically foretelling their future. (See Ibid., 22). The bible "is the only volume ever produced by man or a group of aliens, in which is to be found a large body of prophecies relating to individual nations, to Israel, to all the peoples of the earth, to certain cities, and to the coming of one who was to be the messiah.

Many books have been written by some of the most competent scholars and well-educated individuals providing the validity of the bible. Several are in the bibliography are few listed. In his book evidence that demands a verdict, Josh McDowell, a graduate of Whelton College and Magna Cum Laude graduate of Talbot Theological Seminary, gives us an interesting comparison:

There are now more than 5, 300 known Greek manuscripts of the New Testament. And over 10, 000 Latin vulgate and at least 9, 300 other early versions (MSS) and we have more than 24, 000 manuscript copies of portion of the New Testament in existence today. No other document of antiquity even begins to approach such numbers and attestation. In comparison, the I Liad by Homer is second with only 643 manuscripts that still survive.

Always keep in mind that our suffering must be in accordance with the will of God, and not because of our own ignorance or disobedience to his word, which can result in unnecessary suffering. (See, Acts 9:16; 1 Pet. 4:19); Jonah 2:2.6). Jonah experienced hell (Shelo). Has anyone else experienced hell? Below is one example:

In his book caught up into paradise, Dr. Richard E. By mentions an experience when God gave him a two-minute vision of hell in which he was placed in a pit. He was told that two minutes was all he could endure. He said, "instantly I realized I was a dead sinner being taken to the lowest bowels of the earth. A sense of absolute terror gripped my being". In this pit, small spider-like demons were crawling all over him in total darkness and isolation. He said he knew he would never see another person; he would never get out. Demons would taunt him,

"Damn God! Damn People! And the smell! Herrid, nasty, stale, fetid, rotten and evil mixed together and concentrated. Stinking, crawling demons mentally delighting in making me wretched. My terror mounted until I was ready to collapse into utter hopelessness, crushing despair, Abysmal loneliness. I was an eternally lost soul by my own choosing… The clammy wet walls held me crushed for eternity without escape".

As I have mentioned, there have been others who have experienced hell. I am not unique. However, any spiritual experience should be viewed in light of scriptures.

III.

MY STORY CONTINUES

My life has constantly changed as I responded to events, people, and opportunities. I have been divinely blessed by my creator. I've also made deliberate attempts to grow, to position myself to received, and to reposition myself to receive more.

I have failed and tried again, many times, before making significant progress toward my goals. My mistakes were also my lessons. I gained experience and did not allow my past mistakes to bind and gag me. The boundaries established in my own mind for how I could go were pushed outward. I found the keys to living without limits. Many of us attribute success or failure to fate or some external force. We believe that we have to be in the right place at the right time in order to achieve much like winning the lottery. But success is a direct consequence of our wanting a more abundant life and working hard to earn it, like waiting through the mud puddles of life toward the beckoning sea. I believe that we are called by God to be the very best stewards of all gifts, talents, and opportunities entrusted to us in this lifetime. The result is true prosperity, real success. My deepest understanding of true prosperity came from my past experiences and prison experiences and law library and paralegal courses in the 10-12 grades and 23 years in prison law library and in ministry from age 7 till now 53 years old California and Texas Prison System and other experiences and in the Military USMC.

The Courage to confront-facing your own indifference

Then you will know the truth, and the truth will set you free (John 8:32 (NIV)

What words of wisdom have you garnered? What would you do differently and what would you say to those who feel that they only go around once and feel powerless to correct what may be perceived as less than glowing results?

There is nothing worse than reaching the end of your life and wondering what could have happened, or should've happened, but somehow didn't happen". The sad memories of a lost opportunity have made many people bitter the rest of their lives. Often it is not the fatigue of the Olympic competitor that is debilitating as much as it is the feeling that if he or she had lunged farther, or pushed harder, he or she might have been holding the golden cup of victory as opposed to the bottled water defeat.

Most of us do not want to wander aim loosely, taking life as it comes. We want to take charge of our destiny and see goals accomplished progressively, according to a plan. There are things in our lives that limit us. You can only correct what you are willing to confront. Now, I have to admit, confrontation isn't always something that I enjoy. But I have learned over the years to say what has to be said and face what has to be faced. Many choose to live in a perpetual state of denial rather than do the hard work that is needed to confront issues, weaknesses and inconsistencies in themselves and others.

God will guide you, but only you can take the first step on the exciting journey known as the rest of your life. You can't have a do-over but you can reposition yourself and have a make-over.

You can have a better life. The question is: Are you willing to fight for it? Fate or state?

The question I had to ask myself in those times and now here I am here in prison when I was sinking in a quick and of debt, and going home to stay with my family, sitting here in prison, and also from experiencing sitting in the dark with no electricity, and homeless kicked us of the house, stuck at a family member apartment with my car impound by crime-stoppers by my oldest brother, J.B. Brown, Jr. (his name changed from Jerry W. Brown) and baby sitter, Willie Dean Brown, II, whom later on conspired agreed with the Fort Worth Police Department to set me up with her ex-boyfriend, Harry T. Johnson to have me killed and witnesses conspired as well, and faced with a hungry family and myself struggling to met their needs and no means to feed them and losing job after job was: do I accept this as my fate or simply as temporary state? If it is my fate, then I'm finished and I should give up.

I answered that I was in a state, one that I could fashion, transform, and resist. I did not succumb to despair, but rather preserved.

When I think of this process of choosing state over fate, I think of the life of Joseph in the Bible. He goes through stages. He feels lost in the prison of despair and has to find his gift in order to change his life.

Joseph was the second youngest of a dozen brothers and was his father's favorite. Gifted with prophetic dreams, Joseph is hated by his brothers for this talent and the future his dreams portend. They attempt to murder him but can't go through with it; instead selling him as a slave to traveling foreigners, who take him into Egypt. His sincerity of character and prophetic talent earn him an important role as the house leader for Potiphar. But when Potiphar's wife takes a lustful liking to her husband employee, Joseph resists her advances only to find himself accused of rape and imprisoned.

Talk about being unfair! Our boy Joseph has faced just about every trial imaginable, his only apparent crime being that he is a gifted man of integrity. But his ability to interpret dreams soon reaches the ears of the Pharoah, and faster than you can say reversal of fortune, Joseph find himself second in command of the entire country. He prepares for the upcoming famine and lives to see his family, whom he forgives and embrace, reunited. (For more details of Joseph's life, see Genesis 37-50).

Joseph was bound by his circumstances. But he overcame them by using his gifts. He transcended from the mundane to the miraculous. It so easy to become engrossed in one circumstance and lose sight of the limitless power that lies within what we have been given. Like Joseph, it's vitally important that we recognize how tremendously gifted we are. It is through understanding the power of your gifts that you can escape the prison of despair. Imagine what would have happened if Joseph had stopped using his gifts just because he was in a prison. He would never have been released he would not have prepared Egypt for the impending famine, and countless laws would have been lost.

Do you find yourself in a situation that could be improved by using more of the resources you have at your disposal? Joseph found himself incarcerated until he discovered a new way to apply his abilities. He re-created himself in a time of need to provide a service. He repositioned himself from convict to miss loner. He couldn't accomplish this, though, before he realizes the position he was in at the beginning. You have to identify who you are and where you are in order to find your gift, your voce. You must speak up and gain your power to move beyond the present prison even if it involves confronting a situation that has left you feeling degraded, demanded, uncertain and irrelevant.

Vision, so crucial to this process, is often one of the first powers we lose when despair sets in. We must not be discouraged by lack of finances and felt defeated. We must motivate ourselves to believe in ourselves of his or her abilities so that we could see ourselves achieve our full potential. You and I cannot achieve what you and I cannot conceive. We can think our thought of our problem was lac of finances, but know I knows that it was lack of vision. We must locate ourself. We must not pursue something that really wasn't in our heart. Sometimes we end up going somewhere because of someone in the backseat of the car. In effect, we who are driving have given control to the passenger. Take the wheel of your life now and go where you are meant to go rather than allow your passengers-mothers, fathers, spouses, friends, sisters, brothers, neighbors- to control your destination. Success is not achieving what someone else wants you to achieve. Success is discovering your gift and using it.

Basically, like each of us, Adam and Eve became caught in a riptide of change and were forced to reposition themselves. The Lord seeks them and asks, "Where art thou?' Obviously, he knew the answer to his question without having to ask it, so clearly, he asked for the benefit of his listeners. Therefore, it is essential that every man or women answer the proverbial question "Where art thou?" for men in particular it is often difficult to ascertain where we are, as we often tend to focus on what we do and what we have, which might actually camouflage a deep sense of isolation hiding beneath the façade of degrees, stocks, bonds, church-membership growth, or whatever you and I dream as a measuring stick of achievement.

For men and women alike, this self-analysis is not easily conducted in a society that seldom asks where are you, but largely focuses instead on who are you and how you measure up against others. But if we are to reposition ourselves for a life without limits, then these stages provide an invaluable assessment tool. These five stages are:

1. Revelation 2. Inspiration 3. Formalization 4. Institutionalization and 5. Crystallization

Back to one

Unfortunately, some of us get stuck in stage five and never get out. While others keep going back to the revelation stage and recreating themselves over and over again. The early church fathers kept returning to Jerusalem whenever things went awry; it was their way of going back to stage one again. Congress goes back to the constitution to get back to one. Company staff review their mission statement in an attempt to return to their core values and objectives. Pianists rehearse scales as a warm-up for complicated piece. Or if they're really stuck, they pick up a guitar! A new instrument is sometimes required if we are to escape the crystallized music of the past and create a new melody.

If you are stuck in stage five, as well as we all inevitably are from time to time, go back to one and get a new and exciting revelation and repeat the proves over and over again. I see women who get married after being widowed, while others say there are no good men. The former are women who, like certain companies, keep reinventing themselves and reigniting themselves by taking up hobbies, going back to school, placing themselves in new environments. They remain interesting and passionate by going back to stage one for repositioning. Like mythological phoenix rising from its own ashes, they are reborn again and again. Change the music and change your dance. Do what you can do to open yourself if up to a new revelation of the stalemate you're in. Maybe you pay off old debts. Maybe you begin to date again.

I don't care how old you are, what you've been through or how many battles you feel like you've lost; it's never to late to win the war. For some of you, repositioning yourself will require you and me to rekindle the cold ashes of what was once yours and my fiery passion. You and I will have to allow ourself to hope again and when I get out of prison and to take small steps toward the goal of becoming who God created you and I to be. It may include picking up a new trade or skill. It may mean going back to school or helping someone else who is going. You can help a student with a part-time job or give to a scholarship fund.

There are many ways to get in the fights! I am simply saying that if you are not moving forward, then you are inching backward. Let's get in gear and make some forward motion with the days and strength we have inside of us: "Where do we god from here?"

If you and I refuse to accept, but whatever you and I do, I hope you come away with a sense of how important it is for you and I to acknowledge those areas of our life where you and I have suffered injustice and defeat as I've done here in my book, where do we go from here. I made a list of some not all the events, people, and incidents that I believe and you can do the same that have held you and I back and kept you and I from achieving more. You may want as I have done discussed my feelings with friends, family members, my pastors, and a qualified counselor. But whatever you do, you and I must never give in to despair and bitterly resign yourself to less than you were created for. You and I must take heart and empower ourselves with education, exemplary role models, and the latest information about your and mine desired area of interest.

No matter how unfair life seems or how often you and I may have failed in the past, you and I can still change and improve our life. And not only change, but grow into the best, most authentic version of yourself as well as I we can be. My friend, it's time to stop feeling that the odds in our favor. We know that if they can defeat their Goliath, then it's possible for us to pick up our sling shot and face our giants. (See Col. 4:1).

Joseph's maturity, burn of suffering, serves as a model for us. To his brothers, he said, "you intended to harm me, but God intended it for good to accomplish what is now being done, the saving of many lives" (See, Gen.50:20, NIV).

Money is the answer.

We've all heard that money can't buy happiness, that it can't buy love, and that you can't measure true wealth. While I believe all of these notions are true, I do know what the bible says about money, and it may shock you. My guess is that most have heard that the love of money is the root of all evil (see 1Tim. 6:10), and certainly greed for and the idolatry of material possess long can easily pollute our motives   and corrupt our hearts. However, as we plunge into thinking through the role that money and material means play in how we reposition ourselves for success, I want us to consider in very practical ways, what money can buy us and what it cannot.

First of all, according to scripture-and here's what may shock you-money is the answer to everything. Yes, you read that correctly! In ecclesiasts, an inspired meditation on the meaning of life; the preacher writes:

A feast is made for laughter, and wine makes life merry, but money is the answer for everything (See, Eccl. 10:19, NIV)

But think about it the preacher is not saying that money will make you happy or fulfill you or me or bring you or me peace and contentment. He simply says that it's the answer to everything; any "thing" that can be had money can provide you.

Money answers everything because usually the larger the sum of money, the more options become available. There's nothing wrong with acknowledging that life is easier and more comfortable if you have the finance resources to grease the wheels of daily life (see Phil.4:11-13).

In 1998 my brother, Rev. Brown kicked me and my ex-wife, Gena out of the house because she told him about the dreams we had about his daddy, that when I had no place to go and we broke into his church to sleep and he knew it he had an alarm system built in it and it went off. My ex-wife, Gena told me my brother Rev. Brown wanted to have sex with her looking between her legs and my brother's wife, Ella found our he was having an affair with this young girl down the street and his wife, Ella, found out and confronted him and my brother Rev. Brown wanted to kill her one night when I came home from a night club. In 1996, while in prison at the Boyd Unit in Teague, Texas where I met my mother's, Q.T. Brown ex-boyfriend, they call him popey whom revealed to me that my mother Q.T. Brown whom I called my sister were my mother because they had a fight and she had a miscarriage and she wanted a little girl but she was very young about the age 12 years old when she had me and gave me to her mother Willie Dean Brown, I; In 1996, when I arrived at the Boyd Unit in Texas Prison System while I was lying down in my cell, a man came through the cells door and I noticed he were very old-in-mid-50's and the closer he came the more my body became hot and I couldn't move my head, but only my eyes and when I called on God in Jesus name that when I could move my head and talk and as soon as cells door open up I went and talked to some fellow prisoners and whom I knew and asked questioned about what just had happen to me and in what, who live in the cell. Someone told me that a prisoner died in that cell and I immediately placed my request to be moved to another cell. About in 1977 we were living in Compton, California 1524 S. Haskin Ave., Compton, CA. On evening me and my mother, Willie Dean Brown, I. whom raised me had an argument and I went to bed anory at her and at that time my uncle her brother was living over for the night and he saw my daddy coming to visit me and her walking through the house and put his hand print on her thighs and left and I almost ran out of the window until he caught me saved my life and I went and asked her to forgive me for what I've done that night. My uncle they call him uncle Bayman, uncle Bayman told me your daddy came and visit his children and his wife and you need to place a bible under your pillow and he will go away. In 1989, when me and my ex-wife slept in my car a t-bird in Compton, California Blvd. and Central Ave. and at that time my manager mistreated me very bad when he refused to let me go on brake and treated everyone else good, as I prayed to God and mediated on things and the matters, doors opening, food flipping on the girls, lights off and on in the store, etc., And then my manager asked me to have my angles to stop it and he pleaded with me and that I could do anything I wanted to do and take as long time on break as I like.

Later on, I stopped my meditations and I quit and never came back to that store again because God told me to come back here to Texas for my children and grandchild and some other reasons God knows best in this matter. We must give people as much chance to adjust to our return as I did for them to adjust to my departure.

We must just remember that we must incorporate my family and loved ones each and every stage of yours and my life, whether its ascending, leveling off, or descending. We must learn to take the excitement of our career and public pursuits into our home and share it with those who are committed to me and you and our well-being. They want to be a part of whatever it is you or me are going through if you or me will only let them. We must focus on relationships before market reports, time with the ones we love instead of time with ones you and me can barely tolerate.

Every eagle lands sometimes. Sooner or later, even soaring wings will grow weary and the eagle will want to land. Don't try to land too fast. Only God, who sits in the control tower, can show you how to realign what you or me did in the air with who you or me are at home. It is through his grace and direction that you and me will be positioned for a safe and satisfying landing. I am not speaking of dying here, just landing. Landing into the welcome arms of a life that is define by more that you have accomplished. I am talking about someone who waits for you and sees you as more than what fans and co-workers see. These are people not colleagues who love you for what you do. Therse are people who value you for who you are. It is with them that you want to land. Part of the reason that the Lord blesses us is we can bless others.

IV.

Who knows how many lives would have been lost if not for the skilled performance of the many female surgeons who have added to the intellectual bank of medical prowess once available only from men> Or how many buildings would be missing from our cityscapes if it were not the graceful designs provided by female architects? Women who grew up playing with Susie homemaker sets are now designing space shuttles for NASA. They have put away the hopscotch games of past years and developed computer programs that have revolutionized many industries.

Certainly, there are great women and renowned ladies who still find fulfillment in traditional roles of mother and wife; they are the domestic goddesses to someone's dream. There is absolutely nothing wrong with that choice. But women have a choice now and not a sentence given by a jury of men. Irrevocable change has taken place, I bet slowly and gradually.

One need not to be a history scholar to know that there was a time in this country when women were not revered or respected as they currently are today. Sexism isn't over anymore than racism is over, but we cannot deny that opportunities and attitudes are a lot better today that they were yesterday.

These changes cannot be appreciated without considering how this new climate evolved; the history of this great nation is not without its blemishes. A male chauvinist mind-set was not unusual when this country was founded, but that doesn't exonerate those who considered women little more that property owned by men or kept in waiting for a man to claim. Women who were not chosen by men were mocked as old maids and treated with some disdain even by other women.

The right to vote didn't come easy for women. Women like Susan B. Anthony and Elizabeth Cady Stanton led the way in fighting for long-overdue rights, including the right to vote. They fought for long-overdue rights, including the right to vote. They fought ardently and fervently to have a voice in government, not to mention the right to run for office, which wasn't even thinkable at the time of their struggle. Domestic violence did not exist as a term, and men often punished women as if they were children. Women had no rights or privileges. No one to tell, no one to confide in. Most women were not even licensed to drive, with few in any jobs available to sustain themselves.

Money, power, and sex became the bartering tools for those who imprisoned the female in shackles both physical and mental! When Betsy Ross picked up here needles and thread to stich the flag, she knew that while she could sew it, she couldn't vote for those who would represent it.

If it was a hardship to be a woman, and it was, one can only imagine what befell women of color. Mary Mcleod Bethune and other black women were astonishing figures of raw courage. They had two strikes against them, being both black and a woman. Neither could stop them from fighting for the rights that are now almost unnoticed, they are so common. But there was a step price paid for women's rights to position and reposition themselves in the workplace, in the political arena, in the financial sector, and in every area imaginable <u>(See Prov. 31:29-30; 14:1; 31:13-29).</u>

$$\mathcal{V.}$$

All of us have people who speak for us. The mother who has a child or a father answering the phone or carrying a message to the teacher has someone speaking for him or her. Your secretary or personal assistant may draft memos or letters for you based on his or her understanding of a certain conversation or phone call. Often those of us in business have midlevel management terms that convey the messages from the boardroom down to the staff and individual team members who need to be informed or who will execute to action points. Inevitably, such people end up speaking for you or me.

Have you noticed the press person who speaks for the president? For an example, Ari Fleischer, who handle the press during the first term of the bush and ministration. Or President Clenton's Press Secretary, Dee Dee Myers, fielding Myriad questions from a variety of journalists.

Don't allow the people around you to run you. It is so easy to do. Don't be surprised or fooled by the challenges that will come from your or my ongoing success. Ohers will try to dump in and steal little bits and pieces of who you and me are or turn you or me into what they want you to be. Some will handle you or me to death, absorbing all they can from the contact. But others will carry you or me, move you or me forward, empower and encourage you or me to remain true to who you or me are and what you're or me about (See Matt. 16:13-14).

Today, some would have us thank that those who succeed must do it all. When in fact both the giver and the receiver have to accept each other's commitment to betterment. To him to whom much is given, much is required. I believe that those who are blessed have a responsibility to help the oppressed; that is not to say that this responsibility relieves the victim of his or her responsibility to be a good steward of those opportunities. But that fact is that both the brother and sister who succeeds and the brothers and sisters who await success are mutually liable. If we do not create an effective brotherhood that transcends our differences and focuses on our communities, then we will never know true joy and contentment (See, 1 Cor. 12:14-17; Matt. 10:39; Mark 14:3-8, Prov. 30:14-15).

Epilogue

Much is required, Where Do We Go from Here?
Comments on hell from some of the "Hall of Fame"

Many people have studied God's word and other resources to understand to subject of hell. Often their study is based on personal experiences of their own or the experiences of others. Often it is carefully researched from animals of theology and historical fact. In my research of the subject after my experience in hell and heaven and of my history experiences, some of these "Hall of Fames" have provided tremendous insight and to support evidence of scriptures of what I experienced for myself in hell. I have provided you with scriptural information and knowledge and my life experiences about hell and heaven as well I gathered during my own research. Without a doubt, what God's word has to say about hell and heaven or about any other subject is the authoritative guide for your life and mine.

As you have been reading my book, you have been able to read many "Hall of Fame" quotes about the topic of hell. These were inserted as additional evidence of the realities of what I saw during my experience. However, you may also find it enlightening to read the additional quotes from "Hall of Fames" included in this epilogue and this appendix included.

The Assemblies of God

There will be a final judgement in which the wicked dead will be raised and judged according to their works. Whoever is not found written in the book of life, together with the devil and his angels, the beast and false prophet, will be consigned to everlasting punishment in the lake which burnet with fire and brimstone, which is the second birth (Matt. 25:46; Mk. 9:43; Rev. 19:20;20:1-15; 21: ∞).

Edward Donnelly

The doctrine of hell should lead us to appreciate more than we do the love and merits of the Lord Jesus Christ... From how much have we been spared?

As our time together in these pages comes to a conclusion, I pray that you have much to give back because of the success that you are enjoying in your life. My hope is that you close this book inspired, encourage, and better equipped to reposition yourself and myself for a live you've and I only dreamed about. So many forces and factors in our lives can inhibit us, thwart us, and slow down and progress toward prosperity in this life and life to come. We must remain vigilant as we move forward, learning from our mistakes and forgiving ourselves and others for yesterday's failures. We must remain true to ourselves and to God and everyone and our heart's dreams, never settling for less than our full potential. Finally, we must look beyond our current definitions of success and ensure that our lives are balanced with blessings beyond career, work and finances.

You must remember that no matter where you are, it's not too late to start over, begin anew, or grow to a higher level. The journey continues.

Even our failures are successes. They represent the miracle that you and I survived. Cause you and I belong at the table and considering what we had to work with, through it looks like failure to us, we survived and our survival has been our success! No matter how wounded you and I are, no matter how handicapped you and I have become, no matter how far you and I are from where you and I could have and should have been-you and I can still make it to the palace and sit at the table with the rest of the king's kids! Yes, even though you and I still have a "problem" tucked under the table cloth that other people cannot see, you and I still belong at the table. It is the command of the king (See 2Sam. 9:1-5, 6-13).

We can no longer allow our past to destroy what God has for us in the present (See Gen. 32:24).

Whether you or me are a preacher, a deacon-black or white- a Baptist a Methodist, a presbyterian, or one of the "boys in the hood", one truth confronts you and me: you and me can never become who you or me want to be until you and me can drop who you or me used to be. The bible says, "faithful are the wounds of a friend" (See Prov. 27:6). If true friends wound you or me, they wound you or me for a good reason. In fact, many times that is the only way you and I can tell a really good friend from a fair-weather friend", one who is only a long for the benefits you or me offer. A really good friend doesn't agree with you or me all the time. No matter how rough and tough you and I act or how mightily you and I roar or how forcefully you and I do our macho act, a real friend will look you in the face and say, "I hear you, but you are still wrong". You won't get any real help from so-called friends until you and I find a true friend who loves you and me enough to stand up to you or me.

We don't have time to play games or fool around and act like little boys and girls. We're too old for that foolishness. "When I was a child, I thought like a child, I spoke as a child, I understand as a child. When I became a man...", we have to commit our way unto the Lord because we don't have time to play games. We don't have time to be "Pentecostal Pimps", or church playboys or church play girls" who ransack churches and cruise choirs for attractive women or men. We don't have time for extramarital affair. We don't have time for sin- we have to make it our reserved seat and learn how to pray for ourselves. (See Gen. 32:25-30) (1JN. 2:13-14).

Brother and sister, there is a demon on assignment that has come against you and me and your family, friends, etc.

Don't allow your job, your marriage, or your ministry to rob you and me of your walk with God- because all else is subject to change (See 2Sam. 21:16-17).

Stagnancy is the enemy of progression. Keep moving. When you learn the art of release, you will begin to expect great things. People only hold onto something when they believe nothing else will come. Don't allow your leaf to wither just because your season is ending! Fruit-bearing and leaf-withering are two entirely different things. Saul left his lead wither when he knew his fruitful season was over. His season had ended and David's was beginning, but Saul could have prolonged his season by obeying God's word. (See 1Sam. 15:22; PS, 1:3).

When you are delivered by God… your old girlfriends or boyfriends are going to know it. So are your old running buddies. And your old drinking buddies. And your co-workers. The people in your old neighborhood are going to hear about it. And for some of you, the people in your church will be able to see a difference (MK. 5:18-20).

Pleasing the father

This is my beloved son, in whom I am well pleased (See Matt. 3:17).

When Jesus stepped down into the Jordan River to be baptized by John the Baptist, he stepped into the fullness of God's purposes for his life. Jesus' step into the Jordan waters was symbolic of his perpetual death and resurrection.

From the shores of spiritual blindness, one might think, "How Awful! Jesus was wading into sin". Jesus was doing so, however, to fulfill the purpose of God-redemption from sin. Jesus was exactly where God wanted him to be, doing precisely what God wanted him to do.

As Jesus stood in the very place God desired for him to stand, God opened up the heavens, the spirit of God descended upon him, and a voice spoke from heaven saying, "this is my son. This is my seed, my son, who pleases me!"

Don't expect God to speak up for you-or to cause others to see you for who you really are-until you are wiling to step into the place where God has called you to be. When you step into that place where you are supposed to be, you don't have to speak up for yourself, fight for yourself, or demand anything of others. God will speak for you. He'll command whatever forces are involved to yield to you, give to you, honor you, listen to you, obey you.

Don't expect God to open up the heavens and pour out his spirit of power and truth and wisdom and righteousness onto your life unless you are where you are supposed to be. When you step into the place God has destined for you, you won't have to take on your own battles, grope about for the right decisions, or wonder if sometimes is right or wrong. God will give you every ability you need. He'll put into your path what you need to have and you won't have any doubt that it's God

who is providing for you or working in you. To please the father...
obey him. Even if it means wading into someone else's muddy waters.

Within every man or women dwells the little child who proceed him
or her. Manhood or womanhood is rooted in childhood. Many of the
thoughts you and I have today come from our early experiences as
children. We court disaster when we carry childish perceptions into
adult relationships.

David showed us the right way to love true friends. He openly loved
Jonathan, without any taint of homosexuality. We're so upright that we
can't even touch one another-except for a slap on the rear after a great
play on the football field. A true man or woman inspires manhood or
womanhood in others.

Do you realize that we all don't heal at the same rate? You or me maybe
healed, but that doesn't mean your wife, your children, your employer,
or your parents have been healed as well. It may be time for you to show
the same patience they once showed you.

If parents have to use childcare support, what kind of help do you
think is best?

State-run facilities rank at the bottom of my list because Christian
teaching is not permissible in public facilities. Children are not led in
prayer before meals, and no reference can be made to God as our friend
and Lord. I also worry more about the possibility of child molestation
in state centers, even though it is rare. For these and other reasons,
I prefer church-run programs that are clean and safe. Even better, if
available, is placement of children with relatives such as grand parents
or aunts or super vision provided by other mothers. Children need to
develop relationship with those who care for them. They should be
left with adults they know and love, if possible, rather than relating to
different employees from day to day in public facilities. (See Ps. 103:13;
Isa. 66:13).

V.

"Seek ye first the kingdom of God, and his righteousness; and all these things shall be added unto you". (See Matt. 6:33, KJV). This is the fundamental principle of life on which all others rest.

The killing of unborn children through medical abortions is one of the evilest occupancies of our time, with 1.5 million babies sacrificed in America as 55 million worldwide each year.

As a general rule, don't risk what you can't afford to lose. This is the way to be successful in life: treat every person as you want to be treated: look for ways to meet the physical, emotional, and spiritual needs of those around you. Suppress your desire to be selfish and to seek unfair advantage over others. Try to turn ever encounter with another person into a new or stronger friendship. Then when this confidence with people is combined with hard work, your future success is assured.

In conclusion:

The universe and everything in it will someday pass away and be made new by the creator. Therefore, the events of today that seem so important are not really very significant, except those matters that will survive the end of the universe (such as securing your own salvation and doing the work of the Lord). God is like a father to his children. He loves them more than they can understand, but he also expects them to be obedient to his will. And he has said, "the wages of sin are death) (Rom. 6:23, KJV). It is still true. Take heart, O man and woman of God! Stand fast in your decision to possess the land and your household will yet yield to the gentle persuasion of the holy spirit. The church and the children of tomorrow cry out for men and women to arise and wage war on their behalf (Joshua 1:9). You and me have been favored by God (See Ps. 41:11-12) (Joshua 1:6). Keep in mind that you didn't arrive in the promise land of your life today of yourself. The same is true for us today. You don't come into your promised land alone. Your acceptance of Christ involved other people and the claiming of your promised land still involves others. Factor is your family. Move as a whole family to the territory God is calling you to claim. Take an inventory today of the things that God is calling you to claim. Take an inventory today of the things that God has promised to you and me in scriptures. (Gen. 4:4-5). Giving to God what he wants and moving the heart of God (Joshua 23:5) because our life has been preserve (Gen. 32:3).

Bibliography

Amplified bible, the grand rapids, MI: Zondervan, 1954, Barton, David. Original intent. Aledo, TX: Wall Builder Press, 2000.

American heritage dictionary of the English language, The New College Edition, edited by William Morris, Boston, MA: Houghton Mfflin Co., 1981.

Great changes occur during the course of my life. But everyone changes. Crime: The simplest definition of crime is "behavior that violates the law". United States laws against crime have their roots in the Old Testament and the English Common Law. Our laws have been written to reflect the moral sense of our community-to tell us what is right and wrong as well as what the government has outlawed, and to further the social purposes for which our community exists.

In the early years of our country, crime and sine were considered very much the same, and criminal laws prohibited various kinds of religious offenses. These kinds of crimes have now been abolished, and we make full freedom of conscience as far as our religious practice is concerned and in many other areas of life. However, many types of behavior are forbidden, and the law imposes serious consequences on those who fail to live by the designated rules of our society. Those who commit crimes are subject to punishment.

As most of us know, each state, along with the federal government, has a large number of laws establishing rules for our society-laws punishing offenses against other people, property, the family and the public. In most cases, when the law is violated, there is a clear offender and a clear victim who gets hurt in an obvious way. Someone does something against the will of another person, group of persons, or their property; and the action violates the law. For example, a teenager may be taken to juvenile courts or referred to child welfare agencies if he or she is involved in misbehavior such as running away from home, truancy, curfew violations, or underage drinking.

The Consequences of Crime: Many of the consequences of crime are obvious, impossible to miss. Just watch the morning or nightly news. A distraught mother or sibling talk about the horror of a child being murdered and a family that will never be the same again. A drunk driver has wiped out the father or mother and bread-winner of a close-knit family. We see sense of young men or young women stealing to feed their drug habit or a Mexican border war over drug distribution and profits.

Causes of crime: Discord and crime of all sorts continue today. To change our life, we need to first think about why we did what we did, because it's almost impossible to change if we don't first address the situation that caused the offending behavior. This is the basics in James 4:1-3 provides the following biblical insight into what causes problems among people. Our perspective has to do with what we believe and how we see the world in which we live. Our perspective is determined by many influences of our life stories-such as the lessons we learned from our parents, the way people around us live, our experiences and education, the way our brains process information, our own self-concept expectations. Because people have different perspectives, they often view the same event or conversation and reach widely differing conclusions about what really occurred-and they often make equally differing decisions as to what is right and wrong in a particular situation (See, 2Chr. 27:1-9; 28:1-27; 29:1-21). Our perspective often determines how we behave in a particular situation.

Confusing needs and wants: Sometimes confusion of needs and wants cause conflict and leads to crime. Needs are what we can't do without. Physical needs would include such things as adequate food and clothing, a roof over our head, reasonable transportation, and other items necessary for our livelihood. Wants are what we desire because we like them or they make us feel better, but they are not essential to our well-being. Our wants might include a popular pair of shoes or jeans, a jazzy new car, eating an expensive restaurant-or drugs to give us a high.

Fortunately, in America nearly all people can get what they need without violating the law. This doesn't mean it's easy or even comfortable for all of us. We no doubt know some people who have great difficulty meeting their needs. They (or their parents if they are children) have health problems, or can only find low-paying jobs, or have been laid off. They are so poor they are barely making it and have to live hand-to-hadith under very difficult circumstances. Difficult as it may be, however, most people can take care of themselves, even if someone they have to swallow their pride and accept help from public or private social services agencies.

One can understand, for example, the moral dilemma of the parent who as a last resort steal mil for a starving baby. The evidence suggests, however, that this type of situation is rare. Many needs exist because a person satisfies wants first. Respect is something that is earned. Respect and self-respect are deeply connected. Self-respect is often defined as a sense of worth or as we respect for one's self.

Hope: Hope is our quiet, never-ending dream for the future. When our present situation is not enough to satisfy our souls completely, no matter how good or bad, we hunger for more. And our unsatisfied search for more is the basis of biblical hope. Hope is not just as wish or want, but is real faith regarding the future. Our faith helps us see God working in our past, see our life as it is, and know that he will work in our lives in the future. Our faith helps us see God working in our past, see our life as it is, and know that he will work in our lives in the future. Think of two women. One is continually abused by her common law husband, and the other has been diagnosed with cancer. The first says, "I hope to beat this cancer". Which has true hope? The one who is being abused has only a wish. She has no real faith and is doing nothing to help God work in her life. The women with cancer pray to God and seeks medical help. She has true hope. (2 Cor. 1:9-12).

When you put your life in the hands of God, you receive hope. We all have problems, and no one is immune from suffering, from hurting others, from being hurt by others, from broken relationships. However, through faith in God we can make the best of our bad situation and hope for a better future.

Responsibility is about cause and effect, and involves behavior and its consequences. Cause is the reason something happens. Effect is also called consequences-is the result. (See. 2 Sam. 11-13) is a good example. Accountability flows from responsibility. A person is not accountable if he or she is not responsible, but is likely to be accountable if he or she is responsible: if he or she caused a conflict, a problem, or a crime. You had a choice in the matter and you have a duty to answer someone.

Peace is a journey: as you read these chapters in my book, keep three things in mind. First, your road and mine to peace will be a journey and not an event. You and I will need to visit and revisit each part, continue to think about your responsibility and accountability, confess when and to whom needed, repent by changing who you are, live a forgiving life, continue to work on your and mine reconciliation, and make restitution as often as needed for everyone to be treated fairly. Second, while these actions are discussed from my experiences in life based on the word of God as I've attempted to put it in a logical order, you may choose a different one. Do what needs to be done when the spirit moves you and me, and don't worry about a particular sequence. And third, remember that some of the actions can be done by you alone, while others such as reconciliation, require action by someone other than yourself or me. Don't feel bad, therefore, if sometimes you or me do our best and still don't accomplish all you and me would like.

Our challenge is to take the journey toward building peace your parents, children, prison guards, medical staffs, wardens, brothers and sisters, yourself, friends and society in general.

Whatever the case, it's clear that alcohol and drugs are so closely associated with criminal activity and much other conflict and bad behavior that they have to be considered as one of the primary causes. They make people too sensitive and confuse their view of reality. They make them try to manipulate and control people. They make them shame-and uncontrolled anger.

"If you are in deep enough, only God can pull you out". And Jesus said in Mark 9:23, "Anything is possible if you have faith". (See. Mk. 9:23). Faith in God works in four important ways: Belief in God lays down a great moral code that sets the standard for our life, it offers hope for attaining that life it demonstrates the total, never ending love that all of us need to give and receive if we are to have peace, and offers a process for changing to a better life. Think about the Ten Commandments, the sermon on the mount, and the golden rule. These three great codes are brought together by the great commandment of Matthew 22:37-39, "Love the Lord your God with all your heart, soul, and mind. This is the first and greatest commandment. The second most important is similar: Love your neighbor as much as you love yourself". (Matt. 7:12; Matt. 5).

Need-love leads people who are spiritually isolate and lonely to yearn for affection from their family, love ones and others. Gift-love is God himself working through a person. It is goodness and a Christian life exhibited in a relationship with another. David reflected on his confession, and the joy of God's forgiveness for his sins against bath Sheba and Uriah in Ps. 32:3-5. We all need to confess to God in our own special way, according to the dictates of our own spiritual tradition. Using David as a model will help us. As we pray to God and confess what we're done (Ps. 51:1-6) See also, Famed Psychiatrist Dr. Carl Jung described the value of confession in the problem in modern psychotherapy. See also in his famous satire, the Screwtape letters, Theologian, C.S. Lewis. (New York: Harper Collins Publisher, INC. 1942), P.66).

In sort restoring peace has given me and you tool to use to bring peace into our life, but what we do with them is your and my decision. You and me face a journey that only you and me can travel. You and God working together can attain that better future. The important thing is for you to take the journey and I already took the journey that's why I am writing my book, Where Do We Go from Here.

Acknowledgements

First and foremost, we give all thanks, honor, and glory to our Heavenly Father, God, Jesus Christ, and the Holy Spirit. Without Him, this journey and this book, *One Journey to A Final Destiny*, would not have been possible.

We are deeply grateful to our publisher, Aiah, and her dedicated team, for guiding us, praying for us, and standing by us every step of the way. Your support has helped bring God's vision for this book to life.

We thank our spiritual mother, Leno Scott, for her wisdom and guidance. We will never forget the invaluable help of K.T., our website friend, for supporting us and helping spread the word about our book. To our friends Ann, Kameisha, and Lady Bee Watkins — thank you for supporting our GoFundMe. To our family and friends who prayed for us throughout this journey, your encouragement has meant more than words can express.

Finally, we thank God for each other. For six years, we have walked this journey together, supporting one another in faith, love, and purpose.

Many blessings to all who have been part of this journey.